THE MERCURY TRANSITION

How to Escape from Lifetime Security
to Follow Your Impossible Dream

THE
MERCURY
TRANSITION

Career-
Change
Empowerment
Through Entrepreneurship

Kenneth Atchity

Cover design by Mike Stromberg
Interior design by Donna R. Miller
ISBN: 0-681-45248-X

Printed in the United States of America
First Edition
0 9 8 7 6 5 4 3 2 1

For Chi-Li Wong
"Rocky"

I used to think people doing things weird were weird. That was before I realized that people doing things weird weren't weird at all. It was the people who were saying they were weird who were weird.

—Paul McCartney

The best way to predict the future is to invent it.

—Alan Kay

I think the only immoral thing is for a being not to live every moment of its life with the utmost intensity.

—Jose Ortega y Gasset

Dream abides. It is the only thing that abides. Vision abides.

—Miguel de Unamuno

ALSO BY KENNETH ATCHITY

In Praise of Love

Eterne in Mutabilitie: The Unity of *The Faerie Queene*

Homer's *Iliad*: The Shield of Memory

Sleeping with an Elephant: Selected Poems

Italian Literature: Roots and Branches

A Writer's Time: A Guide to the Creative Process,
from Vision through Revision

Homer: Critical Essays

Cajun Household Wisdom

ACKNOWLEDGEMENTS

Writing this book was a constant reminder of the people in my life who taught me about creativity, and of my own supportive "inner circle" who inspired, protected, and encouraged me during my own career transition. I've been fortunate to have had sterling mentors, including Gayle Delaney, A. John Graves (who's now left show business to become a professor!), Kathy Jacobi, Arpad Kadarkay, Marsha Kinder, Bruce Prince-Joseph, Carol Houck Smith, as well as those who in my memory have now been enshrined as my "saints": Thomas Bergin, Bart Giamatti, John Gardner, Mildred Meyer, Caryl Wickman, Tom Huff, and Norman Cousins.

On a daily basis I'm grateful for generous support from Christopher Borde, Susan Cooper, Alex Cord, Kathy Freedland, Mark Green, Bernie and Lennette Horton, Steven Kates, Sidney Kiwitt, Robert Lawrence, Linda Levinson, Milt Lyles, Michelle Merrill, Shirley Palmer, Wilhelm Post, Mort Ransen, Stuart Robinson, Am Rosen, Mike Schenkel and Marianne David, Terry and Dennis Stanfill, Fred Trester, Alexander Viespi, Robert Wald, Sandra Watt, Steve Weiss, Ellen Weston, and former assistants Tracy Lotwin, Jane Singer, Laurie Parker, Sally Im, Kira Calmette, and Larry Bolton. I'm most appreciative to Sasha Goodman, Barbara

Sher, and Marsha Sinetar for encouraging me to write this book. My clients and students have been a constant source of ideas and responses; and I feel fortunate to have had Pam Liflander and Jo Glorie as editors.

Most of all, for sharing in the struggle and egging me on, my loving thanks go to my mother; son Vincent; daughter Rosemary and her husband, John McKenna; sisters and brother; grandfather James Atchity; Wilbur and Martha Aguillard; and David Adashek. And to the memory of my father, Frederick Atchity, the Accountant now residing within me.

Prologue:
The Mercury Transition

Apollo, the god of reason, gave the caduceus, usually depicted as a winged and golden-flowering rod around which two serpents are intertwined, to his little brother Mercury in exchange for Mercury's wonderful new invention, the lyre. Mercury was known among the Romans as "Mircurius, caduceator" (Mercury of the caduceus). In one

form or another, the golden serpentine winged baton was a powerful symbol in major mythical and psychological arenas. It signified enterprise, commerce, crossroads, healing, reincarnation, sexuality, and the vitality required to face a life of twists and turns. Mercury is the god of transitions. The element named after him is noted for its fluidity.

In another myth, Tiresias, heroic son of the mortal Everes and the nymph Chariclo, was carrying the caduceus when he came upon two serpents mating. He threw his golden rod down between them, and was instantaneously transformed into a woman. Talk about career change!

Odysseus carries the metamorphosized caduceus in

Homer's *Odyssey* when he vanquishes the Cyclops, tames Circe, withstands the serpentine Sirens by tying himself to the mast, survives shipwreck by clinging to the rudder, and slays the suitors who have been exploiting the hospitality of his home. Odysseus looks for trouble because he knows, with his mastery of the staff, he thrives only when solving problems in *transition*. The mercurial Odysseus has turned career transition itself into a lifelong career.

Once you get into the power and patterns of changing, you will probably continue changing for the rest of your life.

To me Mercury's magic caduceus represents the flux of past, present, and future as well as the three parts of the mind (Accountant, Visionary, and Mind's Eye) in their triadic interplay at the infinitely challenging crossroads of career change. The caduceus, in the most general expansion of its mythic metaphor, represents the *technique* or *method* the creatuve personality employs to pursue productively his unique madness. At its most specific, the caduceus is the dollar sign, $.

When astrologers tell me that Mercury is in retrograde, I always take it positively. I figure that my Olympian guide has merely come back to get me so that we can continue our adventure together.

Contents

THE MERCURY TRANSITION

Introduction
"Go for it!"

Jung: Neurosis is no substitute for genuine suffering.

Atchity: Take credit for your pain.

How many times have you felt as if you were hurtling toward a brick wall at 90 mph—and someone supposedly dear to you gave you the advice, "Slow down!" or "Relax!"? As many times as I've been advised to slow down, I've wondered whether hitting the wall at 30 mph was truly preferable to hitting it at 90. If you're going to go splat, let's make it a complete splat!

How else will you find out in time whether that wall is in fact, as you imagined, a secret door to your dreams?

This book is about the speed of your creative life—and about the wall which so often becomes a door. Your chosen speed and trajectory are precisely what distinguish you from the others who are saying, "Relax."

If you're one of those fortunate souls whose attitude is always perfect, who goes through life with an eternal smile of confidence, and who has never found it necessary to scream or to cry, this book is not for you. I wish I could say, through the years of my career transit, I've always been "up."

The truth is I've had to build my "upness," sometimes from what felt like scratch, nearly every day. I like to think it's because the life I've chosen requires me to do things I've never done before and I'm not always certain I can find a way of doing them.

"What makes you an authority?"

Einstein: The punishment fate has given me for my hatred of authority is making me one.

Atchity: Authority comes from seeing that everything has a clear pattern in retrospect.

A few, very long years ago, I resigned my position as tenured professor of comparative literature and mythology at Occidental College in Los Angeles to pursue a new full-time career as free-lance writer, independent producer, teacher, and literary manager. I exchanged a 30-year "comfort horizon" (the comfort horizon is how much of the future I can see as being covered by income-generating contracts presently in hand) for one that has, since then, ranged from a mere 24 hours to, at the very best, nine months—and normally hovers precariously between 45 and 90 days. When people tell me that my mid-life career change was insane, I remind them (and myself) of Salvador Dali's observation: "The only difference between myself and a madman is that I am not mad." Anyway, it makes *me* feel better.

My decision to resign from my tenured position was finalized in the middle of a December snowstorm in Montreal, where I had gone on a leave of absence from

Occidental College to supervise the production of the *Shades of Love* series of romantic comedies for Lorimar and Astral-Bellevue-Pathe. The decision came on the heels of the familiar sensation that everything occurs to me means something: I was scheduled to appear as an "extra" professor in *Sincerely, Violet,* but the snowstorm delayed me and when I arrived on the set the scene had already been shot. I decided that day that I simply was no longer meant to be a professor in fiction or in reality and that it was time to resign.

Although the incident in Montreal provoked action, the decision had been a long time in the making. It had been conceived 12 years earlier, during the year I served as Fulbright Professor at the University of Bologna. On Valentine's Day, I received a telegram from the Occidental Dean of the Faculty telling me that I'd been granted tenure. My immediate reaction to this news surprised me: I became depressed. My depression continued for at least a year, compounded by my difficulty in finding colleagues who could relate to this bizarre reaction. I should have been ecstatic. Finally I figured it out for myself: I felt trapped, and suffocated. My oldest recurrent nightmare as a child was of being suffocated by an enormous blanket not of my own weaving. Yes, the cage I was in was a golden one; but it was a cage. As much as I loved teaching and had done well at it, I had trouble with the concept that for the next 39 years I'd be able to predict my schedule 12 months in advance. I felt that I was out of control, that my life was coming to an end, and that I'd turned myself prematurely into a zombie. I knew I had to escape somehow.

At Occidental I'd created internships that allowed students to work at film studios, newspapers, and publishing companies "in the real world." As I lectured on creativity and writing on campuses throughout the country, somehow I was feeling more and more "dishonest" about the safe life I'd chosen for myself. Until I realized two things.

1. I hadn't really *chosen* to be a professor. I'd simply responded to the job offers I received when I left graduate school by accepting the most attractive one in a place that was most conducive to raising my young family. I'd also imagined that being a professor meant teaching all the time, never foreseeing the realities of committees, bureaucratic red tape, and endless campus politics.
2. How *safe* was the academic profession? While tenure was a magic word for some people, I knew that the economic realities were such that even tenure would not be immune should the college find itself in financial straits. I realized that the safety my colleagues valued so highly, was, more accurately, the *illusion* of security. I'd never been comfortable in a uniform and being a professor was, complete with tweed jackets and leather elbow pads, a uniform.

I also realized that I preferred the illusion of freedom to the illusion of security. When I talked about my restlessness with novelist John Gardner, who was at the time editing my first book on Homer, he told me I was crazy. That I should remain as a professor, doing whatever I wanted to do from that secure foundation. As a creative entrepreneur himself, he very wisely could not recommend his lifestyle when he compared it to mine.

So I hung on another year or so, satisfying my restlessness by founding and editing "off-campus" magazines and an arts newspaper. Then I had the good fortune to encounter Norman Cousins, whose columns in *The Saturday*

Review I'd read growing up. No doubt reflecting the mood I was in, I was offering a course that year entitled "Literature and Death" and, inspired by Cousins' *Anatomy of an Illness*, invited him as a guest speaker. He accepted. During his presentation to my class, Norman used Ortega y Gasset's observation about intensity quoted on the opening page of this book. I was stunned, never having heard anyone else cite these stirring words. After class, I asked him if he'd stop by my office for a minute on the way to lunch at the Faculty Club. I wanted to show him the plaque I'd hung above my desk, bearing the same words. On the way to lunch, I asked Norman if I could take some of his time, at his convenience, to talk with him about "what I should do when I grow up." He laughed, and asked me if I played tennis.

A few days later, to my surprise, he called to ask if I could make the fourth in a doubles game. After a rousing game, Norman listened to my achievements, dreams, and ambitions, and gave me several pieces of advice.

"Whatever you do," he said, "don't ever give up your diversity." I couldn't believe my ears. All my previous advisers had consistently said the opposite. When I had proposed the idea for *Dreamworks* (an interdisciplinary journal devoted to dreams, myth, the arts, and creativity co-founded with my Occidental colleague Marsha Kinder) to Paul Chance at *Psychology Today,* he'd responded with a long, thoughtful letter criticizing the magazine's diversity and actually ending with the words, "Find your niche, young man, find your niche." All my life I'd been looking for my niche among the niches defined by others. Norman was advising me to *create* my niche, defining it with sufficient diversity to replace the suffocation response with excitement and hope.

His second suggestion threw me for a loop. He told me

that the best place to exercise my particular talents and ambitions was the entertainment industry. When I told him I knew nothing about it, he recommended that I read William Goldman's *Adventures in the Screen Trade* (Goldman's scripts and novels include *Marathon Man, Butch Cassidy and the Sundance Kid,* and *Magic*). I knew I had found my second career when I came to Goldman's "single most important fact" of the entire movie business: "NOBODY KNOWS ANYTHING."

By the time I'd finished Goldman's book, I was convinced that I didn't want to go into my second career *only* as a writer. Writers have so little leverage until they've established that unless they're lucky they could wait forever to be recognized. I didn't want to rely on luck, and I didn't have forever. I realized I needed to learn enough about the industry so that I could produce (having little idea of what a producer does). At that point, serendipity came to my assistance in the person of A. John Graves, who was taking a graduate course I was offering at California State College at Los Angeles on "Shakespeare's Ten Worst Plays."

John had been an executive at NBC and was now working as an independent producer. He approached me after class one night and asked if I'd thought about a career in show business. I couldn't believe my ears. A few lunches later, I had the mentor I needed and a desk full of contracts to read (my theory was that learning a new business would go faster if I started with the endpoint of a deal). I read every contract I could get my hands on, including one that included, "Accounting terms shall be defined in such fashion as the Twentieth Century Fox accounting department shall define them at such time, if any, that litigation is entered into among the parties." Although I would wrestle with the concept many times in the future, I had just encountered for the first time what's known in "the biz" as "creative accounting."

Four years later, when *The New York Times* had printed a full-page story about my Lorimar-Astral series of romantic comedies, I bumped into my mentor in a former life, Bart Giamatti, in the elevator of the New York City Yale Club.

"Atchity," he said, "What's this I hear about a professor of comparative literature producing romance movies?"

"What's this I hear about the President of Yale becoming the Baseball Commissioner?"

"Touché," he laughed.

In making the move from security to freedom, substituting an illusion I prefer for the illusion that was suffocating me, I had initiated a full-blown mid-life crisis. If I'd taken the ten-question "stress test" two years after I resigned from Occidental, I would have set the record for "major life changes." Within three years, I'd changed jobs, homes, cities, spouse. And my father died.

In the midst of one particular crisis in my brilliant new career, I found myself in San Francisco, at the home of dream therapist Gayle Delaney (*Living Your Dreams*). Gayle suggested that I incubate a dream to determine whether I truly thought I had within me the resources to continue along the course I'd set for myself. I dreamed, *I found myself between two apparently equal serpents, and realized they were in the process of devouring me. But they didn't.* I woke up elated.

"What do you think the serpents represent?" Gayle asked the next morning.

"My problems? My conflicting motivations?" I thought about it, realizing that they must relate to my theory of the two parts of the mind in constant war with each other. By the time we'd worked it out I realized that the dream was related to my lifelong fascination, as a student and teacher of mythology, with Mercury's caduceus—flowering rod, plume, and serpents (although some representations show only one serpent, I've always favored the ones with two). But the snakes in my dream were the Past and the Future, with my own personal skills in the midst of them in the Present, managing to stand upright. The Past was trying to pull me back into it, the Future, with all its fears and anxieties, was determined to devour my energy. But I was safe in the Present moment because the center of safety lies in the centered self that has learned by mastering itself to master the world. As a student of the *Odyssey,* I recognized the mythic origins of the dream as related to the Greek concept of *techné,* the protean virtue of Athene and Hermes (Mercury) whose mortal counterpart is Homer's hero Odysseus. As Odysseus was able to vanquish the serpentine monsters encountered on his embattled journey to Ithaka, I would be able to master the dragons threatening me from both sides.

The dream told me, in other words, that fighting dragons was my natural profession. No wonder I was, despite my high anxiety, essentially content with my decision. My contentment had reached its height one blizzardy day on a flight between Montreal and Toronto when the prospect of the plane going down in the storm didn't concern me enough to make me look up from the script I was editing. At the time we were still shooting a film in Montreal, but were already in postproduction at Pathe's sound lab in Toronto. A "final mix" was scheduled that night (where the music was being added to the film's sound effects). Everyone thought I should skip the mix because of the weather, but I went to the airport because I was determined to master every detail of my new career. At Montreal's Dorval Airport, I discovered that Air Canada had canceled its flight to Toronto because of the storm. But a smaller, prop-driven airline was leaving in ten minutes. I decided to take it, ignoring the fear of flying I'd previously experienced.

As the plane lumbered through the snowstorm, it occurred to me that I didn't mind the thought that I might die on this flight. I was living my dream, and a happy death would be dying in the middle of my dream. Elizabeth Kubler-Ross's studies of death and the dying found that people "are not afraid of death per se, but of the incompleteness of their lives, of dying prematurely."

There, on the plane, I felt my life was complete. I also realized I'd have to expand my dream to give me reason to continue living with this wonderful feeling of fulfillment.

I began to accept that my view of success isn't about garnering achievements so much as about *achieving* (in the words of Robert Browning, "Ah, but a man's reach should exceed his grasp,/Or what's a heaven for?"); and that this view made me different from many of the people who, along the way, applied to me for jobs, consultations, and conversations about "how to do what you did." Listening to them, consulting with them, I could see that it was product, not process, that turned them on. I began to see that whether they are salespeople or athletes, writers or inventors, builders or proprietors of boutiques, entrepreneurs—Type C personalities—are quite different from others. They are in love with the words, *"Go for it."*

People regularly say that it "took a lot of courage" to resign the total security of a tenured position. The comment at first sounded alien to me, then started to trouble me more and more. I always liked to take credit when I do something good, and "courage" does sound good. At one point, at Marsha Sinetar's suggestion, Dr. Joyce Brothers and her television crew came to interview me about career change. I remember it being a day of the usual crazy pressures, but I did my best to talk sensibly about why I made my own transition and what it felt like to be in the middle of it. Dr. Joyce kept saying it was "courageous," and I kept changing the subject to worrying about "the wolf at the door." But a few months later when the program aired, I had to admit I was impressed with how my story looked from the outside. One of my fellow interviewees was a hairdresser who'd gone after her medical degree in psychiatry at the age of 40-something. Earning that credential allowed her to exchange listening to clients for $25 an hour to listening to them for $125 an hour. Another was a man in his eighties who was just receiving his law degree. It was his *fifth* career change. He recounted his experience on registration day.

"The young man behind me in line finally asked, 'Sir, may I ask you what you're doing in this line?'"

"What line *should* I be in?" the octogenarian answered.

I could see why what I had done appeared like courage to others. But I didn't feel courageous. Often, instead, on those many mornings and afternoons and especially evenings when I had absolutely no idea how I could continue for another hour, I felt certain I'd made a gigantic mistake. I reasoned that, had I foreseen what it would cost me in every aspect of my life, I might never have undertaken my "brilliant" new career. Visualizing the future is one thing. Actually *seeing* it would have discouraged me.

Instead of "courage," the word I came to use was "challenge." I needed to feel *challenged*, needed to *challenge* myself. My career transit was a necessity, not a luxury, keeping my sense of "self" intact. Did I have the strength and stamina to face the unfamiliar adversities I chose for myself? And to be called, in the process, "self-centered," "selfish," "crazy," and "irresponsible"?

Sophocles; It's a terrible thing to look upon your troubles and to realize that you yourself and no one else are responsible for them.

Atchity: It's a wonderful thing to look upon the challenges I've created for myself and to embrace them as my own.

Let's admit that it takes courage to live with the consequences of your decision to be yourself—however you conceive yourself to be. It takes courage to stand apart from and against all the "normal" people out there who criticize and raise their eyebrows, wondering why you're so crazy (while they wonder, to themselves, why they can't be a little more like you). But more than that it takes courage to stand against the enemy within: the normal person inside you, shaped by your parents and the Society of the Non-weird— who spends all his waking efforts trying to stop you from doing anything as insane as quitting a high-paying, secure position to pursue your idiosyncratic need for freedom, creativity, and self-definition.

Career transit isn't recommended for the overly critical or for those who need security. Career transition is for those who know that the ultimate arena lies in the self-knowledge that comes only when you pit skills beyond your present imagining against the relentless resourcefulness of a world of troubles. Theodore Roosevelt was such a man.

It is not the critic who counts, not the man who points out how the strong man stumbled, or where the doer of deeds could have done them better. The credit belongs to the man who is actually in the arena; whose face is marred by dust and sweat and blood; who strives valiantly; who errs and comes short again and again; who knows the great enthusiasms; the great devotions; and spends himself in a worthy cause; who, at the best, knows in the end the triumph of high achievement; and who, at the worst, if he fails, at least fails while daring greatly, so that his place shall never be with those cold and timid souls who know neither victory nor defeat.

Roosevelt makes "risk taking" and "being creative" sound glamorous to those who haven't gone for it. He, and those who have, know better. No one in his right mind would encourage anyone over the age of 25 to sacrifice security for the unknown country of a new career.

But if you feel the need to change, if you're one of those people who long to live the creative life, this book might help you chart new territory. Francisco de Goya complained that "the sleep of reason produces monsters." This book may help you deal with the monsters of your imagination and of the undiscovered country down the road not previously taken.

The ultimate investment is investing in yourself—by designing a life around your unique interests. Everyone tells you that's the way to happiness, but very few people encourage you to pursue such selfishness—and even fewer pursue it for themselves. Those who do are the ones who make a difference. When creative career change is successful, it leads to fulfillment. But when it's not? When you get into it, you begin quickly to realize that "success" is ephemeral. Not simply because change is tough, but because even the word "success" must be redefined in order to continue being useful. I didn't feel successful after *having produced* my first 16 films, but I felt very successful while *producing* them.

Aside from suffocation, my greatest fear in life had always been feeling that my energies weren't being challenged, that my time was being wasted. I'd reacted strongly to the poignancy of Lyndon Johnson's telltale comment: "To hunger for use, and to go unused, that is the greatest hunger of all." The person who engages in career transit has decided to create that need for being used and useful for himself, following in the footsteps of Bernard Shaw who wrote 41 of his 52 produced plays after age 45—*Pygmalion* at age 57, *Saint Joan* at age 67, and *Buoyant Billions* at age 91. Shaw wrote:

This is the true joy in life, the being used for a purpose recognized by yourself as a mighty one; the being thoroughly worn out before you are thrown on the scrap heap; the being a force of Nature instead of a feverish selfish little clod of ailments and grievances complaining that the world will not devote itself to making you happy.

Everyone's first career is an accident. Your *next* career, the child of your choice, is your mighty purpose that makes life worth living.

K.J.A.
Los Angeles
January 16, 1994

1
Our Troublesome Type C Personality

Dad: Don't take risks.

Mom: Go for it!

Oracle of Delphi: Get to know thyself.

Atchity: One at a time, please. One at a time.

My father, bless his soul, was probably the classic Type A personality—a workaholic whose favorite way of spending the evening was disappearing into his den downstairs to work on his "books" (he was an accountant). No one ever heard him say he *loved* accounting. As far as he was concerned, accounting was simply what he had to do. As he worked his way through life, he kept postponing the gratifications others urged upon him—trips to Europe, driving trips across the country, a shopping spree to enjoy some of the money his hard work had accumulated. He was a child of the Depression, and of an entrepreneurial immigrant father to whom bankruptcy was no stranger. Security was my father's primary motivation. Even when security was no longer a real issue, he continued to work as though it were. The sad part was that work was to him a means to an end, and, except toward the very end, he rarely took time to enjoy the ends his means had earned him.

My mother, on the other hand, was always urging him—and her children—to take risks. Born on a small farm in Louisiana, she'd come a long way through nursing school and to the big city of Kansas City, Missouri, where she saw all her children through school and some of them through college and graduate school. "If *he* can do it," she told us growing up, referring to a headline or a TV bulletin about someone's achievement, "you can do it, too. Just do it." Once she egged my brother on to sell the most Little League baseball tickets on his team by suggesting that he go floor to floor in all the skyscraper office buildings in Kansas City. He was worn out, but he won.

When my father died, I sat at the desk in his den staring at a wooden block slogan that had been enshrined between his pen set for as long as I could remember: "RISK NOTHING, LOSE NOTHING." I realized that to him the slogan meant, *Don't take a risk.* All my life, I'd read it as meaning, *Risk it!* Only at the end of his life had I learned exactly how his perspective differed from mine.

W. S. Merwin: The story of the hinge is that it is learning to fly. "No hinge has ever flown," the locks tell it again and again. "That is why we are learning," it answers, "and then we will teach the doors."

Sesame Street: One of these trees is not like the other one, one of these trees is different.

I like to think it's because of this inner pull between my Accountant father and my Visionary mother that I ended up with what I call for the sake of shorthand a Type C personality—C for creative, C for caduceus, and, yes, C for crazy. Like the Type A, described by Drs. Meyer Friedman and Ray Rosenman in their classic *Type A Behavior and Your Heart*, the Type C is "hard-driving," highly "time-conscious" and seeks out increasing levels of stress. But there's a crucial difference, one based largely on a higher degree of awareness. The philosopher Jose Ortega y Gasset defines a hero as "one who wants to be himself." In this sense, the Type C is heroic, insisting on choosing only stress that brings him pleasure—the stress caused by pursuing his impossible dream—and also on taking responsibility for his choice. Therefore, once they "get their heads together," and learn to relax (like the Type B), Type Cs thrive on the very stress that grinds away at the Type A.

At its most functional, the Type C personality is the creative personality, obsessed with making visionary dreams come true and, almost always, whether happily or not, paying a price for it on an hourly basis. An old Cajun saying puts it this way: "You have two choices: forget your dreams, or pay for them." The Type C has figured out that, as far as we know, we only live once; and the risk of feeling that you haven't fully lived your life, haven't explored your fullest potential, is a far greater risk than any risk you might face by pursuing a dream that, arguably, may be "insane."

If you're the classic Type A personality, you're an overachiever, workaholic, who is supposed to be overly stressed and in danger of heart attack because you can't stop working and don't particularly love your work. If you're a Type C personality, like the people I've been consulting with for the past 20 years, you're overly stressed because the work you love is on the cutting edge—and is therefore misunderstood and rejected most of the time, leaving you misunderstood and anxious as a result. The Type C embraces Sigmund Freud's conclusion (without, necessarily, embracing Sigmund Freud) that the two fulfilling aims of life are "to work and to love."

At his least functional, the Type C lives up to the reputation he has with others, to those who read the "C" for "crazy." A number of recent studies suggest a direct link between mental illness and creativity. Maybe it was easy enough for Dali to distinguish between himself and a madman, but sometimes the Type C isn't so self-confident. He's compelled to give up the risk-free path of security to pursue the rocky road of dreams; but he's very often unsure of himself as he moves along that road, even when he seems to have succeeded. As other recent studies have pointed out, the Type C considers himself an impostor in the very world he's creating as he goes.

Obviously with this tenuous distinction between creativity and craziness, nothing is more important to the Type C than taking care of his head. Which means finding the key to understanding what goes on inside it: which of those voices I am hearing are sane, which are insane, which are right and which are wrong, which come from my dream and which come from what others would have me do—which to listen to, which to silence at any given moment? The stakes of this self-understanding, the foundation of self-investment, could not be higher. What makes one man or woman wear his creativity to a natural end (Pablo Picasso, Thomas Edison, Henry Ford, Audrey Hepburn), and what makes the John Belushis, Ernest Hemingways, or Janis Joplins end up turning upon themselves so tragically? The crucial distinction isn't between those Type Cs who succeed in the outside world and those who fail. It's between those who are in equilibrium with their craziness and those who are overwhelmed and even destroyed by it.

Shakespeare: Ripeness is all.

Atchity: Awareness is all.

At its best and brightest, the Type C personality experiences exhilaration, laughter, and applause; at its darkest, despair and self-destruction. But Type Cs value awareness above all. What is the difference between a functional Type C, and a narcissist? The Type C is productive, with something to offer the world. The narcissist isn't. And, yes, sometimes it's hard to tell the difference. I realized very early in my career change that the greatest success I could achieve was not necessarily succeeding in the eyes of the outward world, but in understanding the battle going on within me and mastering its forces rather than allowing them to master me.

Along the road of trying to design a life that successfully reflects your creative aspirations and dreams, it's part of the challenge and par for the course that you're mostly alone and regularly misunderstood. People who love to work all the time because they love their work are in the minority and subject to the usual discrimination enjoyed by minorities: fear, backbiting, hatred, envy, guilt trips, etc.—from authority figures, from peers, and from their own inner insecurities. I call these forces "the Accountants." They're always and everywhere ready to judge you where you are right now—when what's most important to you is where you're going. Your parents and teachers and bosses (authority figures) are not judging your progress, nor your potential; they're judging your present reality and past success. The worst of the Accountants will tell you, "People never change," unable to relate to your driving desire to do precisely that. Your friends and co-workers at the "day job" are comparing your ancient Hudson to their new BMWs and are judging that, by their standards, you've failed. When you tell them your dream is more important than your car, they'd like to believe you but can't bring themselves to because of what it would tell them about themselves.

The worst set of Accountants are within: those parts of you that tell you you're not "measuring up" (inner insecurity), judging you against a standard you internalized probably when you were much too young to realize what you were doing. Faced with insecurity within based on doing what no one else around you is doing, with calumniation from your relatives, friends, and neighbors, with rejection from the world you're working *toward*, your spirits, from time to time, may flag. How often? One day I was advising a client to forget about tomorrow, just worry about today. "I'm worried about making it through the next *hour*," she said.

"Okay," I said. "Let's talk right now." And we got her through it, partly because I shared with her a poem I'd written years earlier:

Cracking Up Time

Last week
it was down to weeks.
By yesterday
it was days—hours,
by last night.

Now I make it
through each minute,
fearing
what measures
next.

It helped her to know that her feeling that the end of the world was upon her was not unique to her. The Caucasian mountaineers, according to George Kennan, define heroism as endurance for one moment more. Yes, the feeling that the world is ending happens often to the Type C personality, embarked on what could, for all he knows for sure, be a voyage over the edge of the earth into the abyss.

Practice terminal patience

Technique and awareness allow you to proceed despite that feeling. And my first advice is to be patient. It takes five years, as an entrepreneur friend in New York points out, just to get used to the idea that there's no one out there who can help you as much as you can help yourself. As reading the Book of Job will emphasize, almost nothing can conquer patience. Except persistence. Persistence is patience with a plan. In the words of Calvin Coolidge: PRESS ON.

Form a long-range operating plan

Once you've formed your "operating plan," patience and persistence become one and the same virtue. If you glean from the experience of other dreamers' insights that allow you to shape, strengthen, or maintain your master plan, you'll be well on your way to becoming an "overnight sensation" in ten years or less.

"Though this be madness," says Shakespeare's Polonius, "yet there is a method to it." I've always believed that planning to make it in the long run by firmly laying the proper tracks to your dream goal may make it happen sooner. In any case, whether sooner or later, it *will* make it happen—regardless of luck. You can't build a game plan on luck. Meanwhile, while you're working away, with or without luck, you're working along tracks you know head in the direction of your dreams, inspired by Gandhi's words:

I know the path: it is straight and narrow. It is like the edge of a sword. I rejoice to walk on it. I weep when I slip. God's word is: He who strives never perishes. I have implicit faith in that promise. Though, therefore, from my weakness I fail a thousand times, I will not lose faith.

If you redefine success as striving—as continuous progress toward a worthwhile goal—even if you die before you get to your goal, you will be dying a happy death. And if you don't die, and get to face another round of dragons tomorrow, you'll understand that merely surviving is part of your success. "I'll settle for surviving," you'll say to yourself because survival is the first important step toward achieving your goals.

Embrace action as a long-term goal
Focus your energies by making the successful achievement of your creative lifestyle one of your long-term goals. Then, remind yourself that "nothing can happen to the master plan," no matter what obstacles loom today. Move slowly, firmly, professionally toward your objectives. Before deciding that you're truly upset by a setback, ask yourself, "Does this matter to the master plan?" "Does this truly affect my

dream?" If your goal is to succeed in ten years, or even in five years, how can anything that happens today truly set you off track?

Learn to compromise today
If today forces you to compromise, compromise. But don't compromise with your dream, compromise *within* your dream. Adjust your objectives, not your goals. If the sidetrack you're tempted onto, or forced onto by necessity, heads away from your dream, do your best to refuse its temptation and return to the path you've designed for yourself. No matter what the price. If the sidetrack seems parallel, heading in the general direction you want to go, you may take it.

Resist immediate gratification
Try as best you can to short-circuit the need for short-range, immediate gratification. Or, if you must have it, find that gratification *outside* your dream. Sometimes people remain bound in the shallows and miseries of their lives because they are constantly choosing immediate gratification over delayed gratification. The ability to choose to delay your gratification is the Type C's most powerful tool.

Maintain your perspective
Sometimes, buried in the avalanche of the monsters you've created, you'll think you're making little progress. Find ways to stand back far enough so that you can measure your progress. Creative systems of measurement are all around us. I told myself, at one point, I'd make a film deal by the time my odometer reached 33,000 miles. At 32,000 miles,

the odometer cable broke, no doubt touched by Mercury's magic wand. I decided not to repair it until the deal was made.

"Know thyself"

Them: "Are you out of your mind?"

Us: "Just the opposite. I'm in my own mind. Whose mind are you in?"

The legendary inscription, "Know thyself," above the portals of the oracle of Delphi must have been written for entrepreneurs. Your strongest enemy is not the "No," but not knowing the underpinnings of your own behavior, your own motivations, your own strengths and weaknesses. No self-help medicine can substitute for introspection. It's the essential key to *making up your own mind* which is our daily task. Someone defined insanity as expecting different results from the same actions. Your artistic madness must not take this course if fulfillment is to be achieved along the way. I consider my career change a true postgraduate education because, on a daily basis, it's forced me to confront myself in different ways. A happy life, for the Type C, is inspired by love for his dream and governed by his knowledge of himself. The balanced Type C personality not only has a vision, but also has the determination required to pursue that vision. We're lucky. Most people live in someone else's dream. We get to live in our own.

Self-investment is allowing your uniqueness to define your life, and refusing to let anything else define it. Marsha

Sinetar, in her provocative *Ordinary People as Monks and Mystics*, compares the creative personality's lifestyle to that of a monk. Every part of your life, from the moment you rise in the morning, through the several times during the day when you seriously consider signing up for a lobotomy, until at last you find a way to quiet your demons enough to get a good night's sleep, is part of what should be *your* design. I once lectured, at the international conference for science fiction in Trieste, on what I called *auto-possessione*, "self-possession" as a theme in science fiction. That's what you're aiming for, consciously: to take possession of yourself, expelling all other spirits than your own from the mastery of your being.

Along the way it may help to know that the Type C personality has recognizable characteristics. If you ask, "How do I know for sure that I'm not crazy?" it may help to know that your question is a *normal* Type C question. If you *weren't* asking it, you'd be in trouble. If you're filled with free-floating anxiety as you enter into a new project, you're experiencing the *normal* Type C sensation at beginnings. I always tell my clients "if you *weren't* anxious, I'd be worried about you," reminding them of the Cajun saying, "If you ain't scared, you ain't doin' nothin' important."

2

The Accountant, the Visionary, and Your Mind's Eye

Walt Whitman: Do I contradict myself? Very well then I contradict myself. (I am large, I contain multitudes.)

Atchity: It's time to narrow the multitudes down to three.

How many times have you heard—from well-meaning, and not-so-well-meaning friends, "You're living in a dreamworld!" The confrontation is particularly frightening because you've asked yourself the same question all too often. The practical, reasonable part of the Type C mind, the *Accountant* (my Dad), is *always* frightened when the *Visionary*, with its bright-eyed ambition (my Mom), seems to take charge of the day-to-day routine of living. These two voices are the left- and right-brain serpent dragons constantly at war. Mercury's caduceus takes charge of your dreamworld by allowing you to observe which serpent voice is which. Only then can you learn how to conduct with the master's baton their never-ending dialogue.

The Accountant in all of us is the product of our Puritanical culture that wants us to keep busy: Idle hands are the devil's workshop. The Accountant doesn't trust the Visionary, because the Visionary has no idea even what time it is on the Accountant's clock. Accountants are in charge of synchronizing clocks around the world. The Accountant is the voice which, when it comes to words, keeps the alphabet in alphabetical order. When it comes to relationships, deals, sentences, paragraphs, proposals, activities—all structured matters whatsoever—the Accountant insists on "a place for everything, and everything in its place." The great niche-maker and pigeonholer, the Accountant demands beginnings, middles, and ends (in that order). The Accountant insists on yes *or* no, black *or* white, either/or, 1 *or* 0; without the Accountant, we would have no computers. As far as your Accountant is concerned, a stoplight offers two choices: green for go, *or* red and yellow for stop. If you've slammed into someone stopping for a yellow light recently, you've slammed into an Accountant. The Accountant's primary goal and function in your life is survival first, longevity second, health third. Chocolate *or* butterscotch syrup. At the end of each race, there's only *one* winner.

When it comes to time, the Accountant's allegiance is to every logical ordering device from Greenwich Mean Time to your digitized, waterproof, chronomatic, moon-cycle-sensitive, solar-powered wristwatch—and demands that they be kept in sync by frequent synchronizations. When things work like clockwork, it's usually thanks to the Accountant's knowledge of the inner workings of clocks. The Accountant wants us to believe that he is eternal, ubiquitous, and omniscient. In the days before digital bedside alarm clocks, you could set your clock for 7 A.M., and for some reason, awaken just as the big hand moved to 12—*before* the alarm went off. Now, with digital time, you awaken at 6:59 just before the quartz display announces 7:00. Why? Because the Accountant never sleeps. The Accountant designed and controls your desktop computer, always knowing what time it is whether you're "on" or "off." This dialogue, from a "B.C." cartoon (by Johnny Hart), makes fun of the Accountant:

Caveman #1: "You got the time?"
Caveman #2: "About noon."
Caveman #1: "I'd prefer something more exact."
Caveman #2: "About noon, stupid."

The Accountant doesn't even get the joke. The Accountant hates it when everyone else laughs. The Accountant is relentless, untiring, all-disciplined, retentive. But is the Accountant a genius? No. Is the Accountant inescapable? No. Is he truly eternal and ubiquitous? No. The Accountant controls only "objective" or "logical" time.

The Visionary is that force in the Type C's mind that controls the "craziest" voices, the voices of your dreams. It's Hamlet's "undiscovered country" where brainstorms are the order of the day and light bulbs the order of the night. When it comes to the alphabet, the Visionary reaches into a hat and draws a letter: "Today is brought to you by the Letter M." The poet Howard Nemerov asked, "Who put the alphabet in alphabetical order?" to remind us of the Accountant's *arbitrariness*. Alphabetical order isn't *essential*; it's merely *convenient* to the orderly functioning of society.

When it comes to the pea trick at the carnival, the Visionary cheats: None of the shells have peas under them—or they all do. When asked if he believed that every film should have a beginning, middle, and end, the Italian director Bertolucci paused momentarily before answering, "Yes, but not necessarily in that order." When it comes to stoplights, to the Visionary "yellow" is a challenge, living on the edge: Yellow means, "Go faster!" As for Yes or No, the Visionary has no problem saying "Yes *and* No," insisting on the simultaneous validity of opposing forces. When the little prince was asked if he wanted to take a boat or a train, he replied, "Yes, I would like to take a boat and a train." Why should I choose between chocolate and butterscotch when I want both? Is the Visionary disciplined? Not at all. Words like "disciplined," usually betrayed by their Latin roots, are almost always Accountant-determined words. Visionary words include "yum," "ai-yi-yi," "wow," "kee-yi!", and "eureka." The Accountant may be pompous and ponderous and excessively authoritative, but the Visionary can be mean, surly, and downright disrespectful. Visionaries call Accountants "bean counters," because Accountants call Visionaries "lunatics."

When it comes to the Accountant's "reality," the Visionary response is Liza Minnelli's: "Reality is something you rise above."

It's probably the minority who've chosen to listen to the distant drum of that Visionary voice—dedicating their lives to being "artistic," "bohemian," "inventive," "idealistic architect," "mad dog salesman," maverick, developer, impresario, creative, "different," *weird*—all words the Accountant uses to describe those who refuse to "fit in," who are "square pegs in round holes." "Listen to reason," the Accountants who controlled the day said to Joan of Arc. She refused to listen to reason. She was happier listening to the Visionary voices that possessed her. And she was burned at the stake for being possessed. Looking at it from her viewpoint, Joan was *self-possessed* and had the courage of her visionary convictions combined with enough entrepreneurial awareness to save France and make an eternal name for herself in history. The Accountants said, "You're only a girl." Joan replied, "Lead me to your army."

The Type C's Accountant would be much happier if you'd spend all your available hours working in a lucrative engineering position or in a vested government management job where the Accountant could count on a paycheck on a weekly or biweekly basis. The Accountant likes to know where it's next meal comes from. The moment it figures that out, it wants to know where the meal after *that* will come from, and so on. It's never satisfied, even with a vision of thousands of meals night after night on the same patio at the same grill until you're ready for retirement. Then what will we eat? the Accountant wants to know.

Give us a break, you begin saying to yourself after you've lived long enough to know that meals aren't everything and a pre-planned, 30-year diet doesn't satisfy the soul. Your Visionary wants to speak. The Accountant has been silencing him for all these years, and one of the Accountant's justifications for doing so is that the Visionary speaks with many tongues. The Type C personality has as many ideas as the little old lady who lived in the shoe had children. If these visions are allowed free play, reasons the Accountant, they will flood us with their diversity and disorganization and we'll end up *starving*. Yet the ideas, despite all the Accountant can do to hold them behind the dike, keep leaking out. What to do? Without the Visionary, your life would have no meaning.

Competition, cooperation, and creativity in the triadic mind

Your dreamworld's stability depends on discovering that Accountant and Visionary are not the only forces at play inside your Type C mind. If the mind were truly dualistic, we'd be constantly in conflict with no hope for turning competition into creative progress. But cooperation between the two warring serpents is possible because the mind is actually *triadic*. Like the dialectical process of thesis, antithesis, and synthesis, the internal process by which our mind thinks and acts in the world becomes most productive by the yoking together of opposites. The part of your mind that conducts the self-examination, that 'knows itself,' and maintains awareness on an ongoing basis by watching and observing, is what I'm calling your "Mind's Eye." You can see a picture of your Mind's Eye on the back of the U.S. dollar bill—the mystical third eye that unites the two sides of the triangle.

Your Mind's Eye is well aware of the Accountant's anxieties, and respects them because it recognizes the Accountant's essential role in our physical and fiscal survival. Your Mind's Eye, on the other hand, also recognizes the Visionary's need to dream and struggle to make dreams come true. Your Mind's Eye's awareness is Mercury's caduceus that sets the serpentine yin and yang spinning black and white into the stable dynamism of gray. The Mind's Eye is our onboard salesperson, trickster, acrobat, mentor, ringmaster, lion tamer, alchemist, magician, thief, and negotiator between the forces of nature represented by the two serpents—who agrees the Accountant "stands to reason" and the Visionary "inspires hope." The Mind's Eye understands that forward motion, also called "progress," occurs best when two opposing forces are yoked together so their energies can work in time. The Mind's Eye, having done the research the Accountant's afraid to do, also knows that dreams can have *tangible value* in the real world and that their value will never be realized unless a deal can be struck with the Accountant to let the Visionary out of the cave of imagination long enough to express its ideas.

If the Accountant has been in charge of your mind previously, you're mired in a rut, stuck on the treadmill, dying to break free; you're bored. If the Visionary has been in charge, you keep having great ideas that seem to go nowhere, and are truly beginning to doubt your sanity; you're scared to death. Your Mind's Eye, being the most lucid and helpful of the three parts of your mind as you allow it to take over, also recognizes that *you* (defined, in logical terms, as the integration of the three parts of your mind) can't be happy and productive until a world around you is constructed that allows *the free pursuit of your visionary dream in an accountable way.*

The Mind's Eye master *productive* argument, where the name-calling stops because the arguing parties, in their new "creative *trialogue*," have agreed in advance that the purpose of their contretemps is to clear the air and reach an agreement on how to best move forward using the strengths of both sides of the mind. Based on this underlying contract, the contrary parties are freed to express themselves honestly and directly while your Mind's Eye listens, chooses the best or the complementary, and thanks them for being honest and for cooperating with your desire for progress.

The Mind's Eye has two primary functions in your mind, once it has been awakened and empowered. It *observes* and it *negotiates*. Its awareness that the Accountant is useful and the Visionary is perceptive, that the Accountant is objective and the Visionary subjective, that the Accountant is great at organizing while the Visionary is great at conceiving something worth organizing, is the Mind's Eye's first function.

Mastery begins with understanding, and understanding emerges from detached observation. The Mind's Eye is as fast as quicksilver (another word for mercury). *You*—the real you, the best you, the you you want to be—should be associated with your Mind's Eye, observing what you're doing, what you're feeling, what you're thinking, what you're dreaming. Your Mind's Eye's power comes from its understanding, and its power manifests itself in its ability to turn understanding and awareness into arbitration, dialogue, mediation. Others have called the Mind's Eye "the watcher within" or "the monitor," though such terms are too passive.

"The Accountant has a valid concern," your Mind's Eye tells the Visionary. "If you plane your sailboat all day every day, we will all starve." Your Mind's Eye works out an agreement whereby the Accountant allows the Visionary to plane for two hours daily, and the Visionary agrees to take weekends off and devote an extra hour a day to the "day job" until the boat is done and the voyage ready to begin. Your Mind's Eye enforces this contract, insisting that the Visionary use that remaining five minutes to psyche itself up for tomorrow's two hours by deciding what's to be planed next and carefully putting away the tools. The Accountant also respects the contract by turning its constant worry devices off for the two hours, reasserting itself only at one hour and 55 minutes. If it feels it can trust your Mind's Eye's bargain, the Accountant even *appreciates* going "off the meter" for a spell. It can, at last, take a responsible rest. During that rest, it may even learn to appreciate the value of what the Visionary is up to. But the Accountant will *not* cooperate with the Visionary without a firm contract negotiated by your Mind's Eye.

Your Mind's Eye recognizes that "it seems like yesterday" and it "seems like 20 years" refer to the Visionary's *mythic time* being evoked simultaneously with the Accountant's *chronological* or *logical time*. To the Visionary, whose relationship with that someone is/was intense, the last encounter happened "just yesterday." The Visionary clocks time only by reference to intensity. Lovers live from embrace to embrace, the time between embraces "not counting." Your Mind's Eye rejoices in the richness of your mind that can entertain such contraries at the same moment—even celebrate them, now that they no longer need to be constantly involved in the wars of resolving which time *is* it? Your Mind's Eye creates your *characteristic* time by choosing from the time menus offered by both the Visionary and the Accountant. The Mind's Eye is well-described in a letter written by choreographer Martha Graham to her student Agnes de Mille:

There is a vitality, a life force, an energy, a quickening that is translated through you into action. And because there is only one of you in all time, this expression is unique and if you block it, it will never exist through any other medium, and be lost. The world will not have it. It is not your business to determine how good it is, nor how valuable, nor how it compares with other expressions. It is your business to keep the channel open. You do not even have to believe in yourself or your work. You have to keep open and aware directly to the urges that actuate you. Keep the channel open.

Your Mind's Eye recognizes that the *beauty* or *brilliance* of the Visionary's idea can profit from the *form* or *structure* provided by the Accountant—and keeps the channel open. Mercury is playing his role as *psychopompos*, escorter of souls, to take us where we dream of going because he sees all the Accountant's tricks, all the Visionary's tantrums and spells; and he feels confident that, at his bargaining table, something can be found to please everyone: a "win-win" scenario. Your Mind's Eye is the lead horse in the troika, who says Yes to chocolate, Yes to butterscotch, but, "Let's have a half portion of each to be mindful of the calories." If you're not yet hearing that third, all-important voice in your mind, *listen* for it. Your career change will be expedited. The world created by your Mind's Eye is neither a crazy vision nor a "realistic" Accountant's world. It is your *functional dream-world*.

A therapist I consulted told me: "You have the most amazing capacity for sustaining self-delusion I've ever run across." He meant it as a compliment, he said; but his remark revealed him as an incorrigible Accountant. I switched therapists because, for my Type C mentality, *denial of reality* is the necessary foundation for going beyond my previous capacity to achieve. Defining "deniers" as people who "minimize the seriousness of their condition through hope, optimism, and humor," the psychologist Thomas Hackett has measured their extraordinary ability to succeed and to survive in conditions that defeat those who more readily *accept*.

Dreamworlds are always anxiety-producing to the Accountants of the real world, who are by far the majority, both in numbers and experience. The entrepreneur's Mind's Eye has to map the characteristics of his dreamworld if he wishes to achieve the peace of mind touted by those with regular paychecks. For them, character is created externally, by response to social needs; they've "found their niche." For the Type C, character must be designed internally, responding to his need to externalize his vision and sell it to society; he *creates* his niche. If designing your dream, searching for its fulfillment, and creating your niche seems like an uphill battle, it's precisely because you *are* going against the stream; if it *weren't* uphill all the way, you'd probably be doing nothing creative. "Of course it's hard," Tom Hanks, the coach in *A League of Their Own*, declares to his team: "If it weren't hard everybody'd be doing it. The hard part is the great part." My director friend Mort Ransen put it this way: "It's *always* an uphill battle—especially because we're not always sure the hill is there." The Accountants around you, and the Accountant within you, are constantly pressuring you to "join the group"; "take a reality pill." The Visionary inside you refuses.

The Mind's Eye evolved in response to the human mind's thirst for vision, created to intervene between the Accountant and the Visionary, pressuring them to work together toward productive creative expression—without driving us crazy.

A client of mine started working with me because she realized she'd been letting her life go by in a career that wasn't giving her the satisfaction she craved. She said, "I've been walking around with my head up my ass so long my eyes are brown." The next time someone tells you, "You're living in a dreamworld! Your head is in the clouds," you reply: "That's where I like it. And where, exactly, is *your* head?" Be proud of your dreamworld. It's truly your greatest creation.

Coping with your ambition: energy vs experience

Viktor Frankl: What is to give light must endure burning.

Atchity: The secret is to burn without burning up.

If you have ambition, focused in a dream, you have the ability to cope with the obstacles to achieving that ambition and making that dream come true. It's a question of whether you choose to mine that ability or not. Those contemplating career transit often hesitate because, as their Accountant knows too well, "I'm not getting any younger."

That is perhaps unarguably true to the Accountant, whether the Visionary relates to it or not. But the Mind's Eye points out to the Accountant that for every diminution of energy you've experienced, you've increased your experience. Energy and experience are like the pistons in a two-piston engine. As the energy piston goes down, the experience piston has gone up—creating a balance that allows the older tennis player to keep up with, and sometimes beat, the younger. The self-confidence you've gained from your first career is equal to the brashness you experienced when you were going into that first career. The argument from age is unacceptable. You're capable of changing as long as you believe you can change.

Walking the tightrope

When I returned to Los Angeles from a lecture tour in northern California, a package was awaiting me from my

Mom. I opened it to discover a very strange gift, especially since my family generally gives *practical* gifts. Her gift to me was a clock, although I'd never seen a clock like it before. Inside a transparent plastic box, an acrobat was perched on a ball, his feet moving as fast as they could, his hands holding a balance pole that marked the time. I was amazed, and touched. My mother understood the dreamworld I, by fits and starts, was fashioning; and the tightrope I was walking.

In the years that followed, my doodles further explored the tightrope—that straight line between two powerful opposite forces. On one side of the rope (the future) I drew dreams-come-true, *future successes*:

- the production of my first script;
- a client's book receives a six-figure advance;
- the publication of my next book;
- the long-range funding of my television company;
- a client's book wins the National Book Award;
- a client's script receives the Emmy;
- the funding of my marketing company;
- my script receives an Oscar;
- the first single check for $1,000,000;
- the Malibu beach house; and
- the farm in Louisiana.

But these successful dreams, in green, were surrounded by the red dragons of failure—which, until my Mind's Eye took charge, were high-anxiety red-ink *nightmares*:

- debts from my first excursions into business that threatened to swallow up all my current income;

- The IRS deciding to demand a written report on every single phone call; and
- a further slump in the Los Angeles recession that would chase away all clients and supervising producer's fees.

Both the dreams and the serpentine dragons had allies, angels and demons from the past, that slipped beneath my feet on the tightrope in an area I couldn't see because you can't look directly beneath you if you hope to avoid falling. The dragons were:

- the many projects that came within "an inch" of being realized only to slip away into the ether;
- projects that died on the vine from lack of distribution, lack of financing, or lack of interest on the part of the audience for whom they were intended;
- partnerships that began with great expectations and ended in disappointment; and
- relationships that had been strained beyond the breaking point by the discrepancy between my vision of the future and the other party's inability to continue believing that "the ship would come in."

Those were the red dragons that hunkered around, salivating at the green dreams which they would dearly love to eat for breakfast, lunch, and dinner.

The allies (*past successes*) were equally strong, however:

- books published and well-received;
- films produced and distributed;
- new screenplays written;
- production contracts signed;

- relationships maintained and strengthened;
- debt retirements or settlements;
- avoiding bankruptcy;
- getting both children through college; and
- seeing my daughter happily married.

I could point to these as evidence for hope and continuation. Despite out-of-balance expenses, my gross income had been greater each year in my new career than in my old; my source of ideas was constantly not only increasing but improving; my contacts with distributors, financers, and artists were slowly but surely growing stronger each day. Broken relationships had been repaired. Past execution gave reasonable promise for future expectation.

Behind me on the tightrope were the people I'd identified as my "positive support group," family, personal, and business. In front of me, in the direction I was by necessity always facing, were the next "pay periods"—the 1st of next month, the 15th, the 1st, the 15th. Echoing in the back of my mind was always the question, "Am I gambling intelligently with my talents or am I just plain crazy?" Is this a calculated, or a foolish risk? I repeated to myself and to my support group for their corroboration, as a positive mantra to counter these distracting and terrifying echoes, that all I had to do was continue moving forward. "I have no doubt of my long-term success, if I can continue maneuvering pay period by pay period through the short term."

At moments like this, I recall e.e. cummings' poem about the tightrope walker: "an artist, a man, a failure, proceed." Given that the cliff above is no more hazardous than the cliff below or than the ledge upon which you're standing, your best bet is to continue going for it.

3
What's the Plan?

Epictetus: First say to yourself what you would do, then do what you have to do.

Atchity: Plans make dreams come true.

The most exhausting and most challenging part of my new entrepreneurial life is the constant need to re-evaluate what I call "the operating plan." Even though control may be an illusion and fate may be more important in our lives than our own actions, maintaining equilibrium and "perspective" in a sea of troubles requires a reference point. The reference point is the overall strategic operating plan you've decided, in your Mind's Eye, to pursue. My Mind's Eye has to rally me back to the dream quest by waving the operating plan.

I discovered that if I *don't* do this constant reevaluation, and let myself drift too long, my anxiety starts announcing itself in various parts of my body. Moveable pains signal that I've been ignoring system distress. Having an active Mind's Eye on board has provided insight over the interaction between mind and body I would otherwise not have understood. Here's the pattern I've noticed about myself, the behavior pattern and interaction with the world that occurs when I'm taking a detour from my operating plan. The warnings from my unconscious come in stages.

- Warning Stage #1. First the body pains, usually focused in my lower back. If I ignore them, the pressure on me to notice what's happening accelerates into Stage #2.
- Stage #2, traffic "near misses" (although as George Carlin points out, shouldn't they really be called "near collisions"?). I bump into the car in front of me at a stoplight, ever so gently but enough to wake us both up. I scrape my hubcap against a curb. I hit the bulwark in the garage a little harder than is good for my front bumper. My unconscious is screaming for attention.
- Stage #3. If I ignore those signs, the next stage I can predict is that I'll lose my wallet. If my "detour" is serious, this can be a real loss—forcing me to get a new driver's license (I now keep two spares in my desk drawer for this purpose), cancel credit cards, etc. If it's less serious, the wallet will turn up as soon as I've stopped to regroup. But while I'm looking for it, without having come to the realization that these events are *signs*, my unconscious goes to the final level, Stage 4.
- Stage #4: I lose my glasses. Sometimes three pairs of them within the same 24-hour period. Once I was in New York on business for a few days before taking a much-needed vacation on Antigua with my daughter, who was a sophomore at Columbia College at the time. She stayed at the Yale Club with me the two nights before we were to leave New York. I managed to lose my glasses at a Greenwich Village production of *Steel Mag-*

nolias. Having been through this before, Rosemary patiently accompanied me around to the bar we'd stopped at en route to the theater. No luck. To the theater itself. No luck. I lamented that I'd just *bought* these new "far-see" glasses, but finally gave up and returned to the Yale Club determined to buy another pair in the morning so we wouldn't be visionless at the beach. I asked my dreams to tell me where the glasses were lost. When I awakened the next morning and got out of bed, I almost stepped on them. They were at the pillow-end of the bed, on the floor. The dream answered with a reality, and I felt much better.

In Antigua I lost them again on the beach. This time I didn't find them. Rosemary wanted to know why I was so intent on losing them. "Because my unconscious is trying to tell me something," I explained.

"What?"

"That I can't see where I'm going."

And my unconscious was right. I resigned from the company I was working for the next month.

Now every time I lose my glasses, I reevaluate the operating plan first and look for them second.

An *operating plan*, constructed through your Mind's Eye's negotiation with the Accountant and the Visionary, is the overall relationship between goals and objectives with a built-in "revision factor" along the way.

• You will begin to taste that dreamed-of future happiness in the present when you construct your plan to suit what you now have in hand where you are at the moment.

- You'll have a better attitude toward your day job by knowing that it's now clearly a means to an end.
- You'll be more compassionate with your family's pressing needs when you realize you've found a long-range way of having your own needs met.
- You'll deal with today's financial anxieties better by knowing that you've planned for a profitable tomorrow that *requires* taking a calculated risk now.

Immense relief sets in when you extend your operating plan without limitation into the future; as Cynthia Whitcomb puts it, "Don't put deadlines on your career." Saying to yourself, my dream is to be a shopping center mogul within three years is an invitation to self-sabotage. What you say instead is, I'm going to develop my own shopping center. That's the plan. Then you proceed to set objectives along the way, and to post target deadlines for the accomplishment of each objective—while, at the same time, also posting notices to yourself to revise those deadlines on a regular basis. "In order to hit the duck," says Lee Iacocca, "you have to move your gun." If you set an unrealistic deadline for the accomplishment of your goal, your Accountant won't be convinced no matter how confident your Visionary is, nor how energetic your Mind's Eye. How do we know what's realistic or not realistic in a situation we haven't mastered before? That's precisely the point: we don't, so we can't set hard-and-fast deadlines. Even the Accountant knows you can't become a sensation overnight, at least without extraordinary luck. You accomplish one objective after another until a goal is achieved: you learn what you need to learn, you apply it in a low-risk situation as a test, then you apply it for real, and so on.

If there's no upper limit on the achievement of the goal you've dreamed for yourself, obviously your commitment must be total. It's easier, you'll discover, to make a total commitment to a dream without a deadline on it. But the goal will never happen until you move to the next step in planning: setting objectives that do have deadlines, ones that are both challenging and realistic. An objective is *not*: winning the Nobel Prize, becoming Mayor of Saratoga Springs, or winning an Oscar.

Dreams? Plans? Goals? Objectives? What's the difference?

Dreams are the foundation of your inspiration and energy, the baseline ambition of your Visionary that has led you to take the risks you're taking. They are, in other words, expressions of the guiding *vision*. You can see yourself as the shopping center mogul of Leawood Park, can feel it in your bones, can taste the success—all of this before you've ever even seen a shopping center blueprint.

Dreams come first. And, with the help of an operating plan, you can turn dreams into realities.

Making them come true requires two things: *commitment* and the *plan* itself. Commitment marries your dream to your mission in life; you are going to make your dream your mission. The German poet-philosopher Johann Wolfgang Goethe made the most powerful statement about commitment I've ever run across:

Until one is committed, there is hesitancy, the chance to draw back, always ineffectiveness. Concerning all acts of initiative (and creation) there is one elementary truth, the ignorance of which kills countless ideas and splendid plans: that moment one definitely commits oneself, then Providence moves, too.

All sorts of things occur to help one that would never have otherwise occurred. A whole stream of events issues from the decision, raising in one's favor all manner of unforeseen incidents, meetings and material assistance which no man would have dreamed could have come his way.

Whatever you can do or dream you can, begin it. Boldness has genius, power and magic in it. Begin it now.

Decisiveness, according to Lee Iacocca, is the primary quality of a good manager. But decisiveness is hamstrung without a plan. Now that we've begun, we need a strategic plan. A plan consists of general *goals* (strategy) and specific *objectives* (tactics). Like dreams, plans should contain deadlines, but should not be governed by deadlines.

Let's say your dream is to be a shopping center mogul. As long as you're moving generally toward it, nothing can take the dream away. But the plan recognizes that dreams like this come true step by step, and focuses on the first step: learning about, acquiring, building, or otherwise developing the first of those shopping centers.

A plan consists of *goals,* reached by *objectives* to be accomplished within a specific time frame laid out on an *agenda*. Objectives and goals can have deadlines. Dreams cannot.

Dream: To be my town's shopping center czar.

Current Situation: Working as a teller in the bank.

Operating Plan

Goal: To own and profitably operate my first shopping center as a trial-run within 24 months.

Agenda

Deadlines	Objectives	Notes and "When"
During Month 1	Research continuing education catalogs; 1–2 hours weekly	During lunch breaks
By the start of Month 2	Enroll in evening real estate class	Choose instructor who knows most about malls
	Spend 3 hours weekly surveying existing malls	1 hour during lunch break on M, W, F
	Subscribe to *Shopping Mall-O-Rama magazine*	
Start of Month 3	Revise this agenda	Don't forget to schedule "when"
	Get intro to manager of Century 21	Ask instructor or Jack at H & R Realty
	Visit City Hall to get regulations on malls from planning board	Plan half-day off for this purpose
Start of Month 4	Revise this agenda	
	Tell instructor the "dream"	
	Check on liquidity of CDs	
	Talk to bank about foreclosures	

Your plan will reflect the individuality of your dreams and goals, but don't forget, in that right-hand column, to remind yourself that a "to do" list has limited usefulness without knowing *when* you're to do it. An agenda consists of "things to be done" in a particular time frame.

Note that your second month limits the hours devoted to your dream to eight or nine, including the evening class. Your Accountant is happier when you ease reasonably into the dream quest. You revise the agenda monthly in order to maintain your perspective; the agenda is working for you, you're not working for it. Your revisions will be based on your successes and failures during the previous month. Did you fail to accomplish any of the objectives? Did you fail to spend the time you planned? This month, set your objectives lower so that your chance of success becomes higher. The process is one of constant reevaluation. But between the reevaluations you will do your best on a daily basis to accomplish the objectives you've set for yourself.

When you feel the need for inspiration, go to the library and research "success stories" in your own field. You'll discover, more than likely, that the men and women you'd choose as models for your own brilliant career moved toward success through a series of what others would define as failures—and constantly revised their perspective toward what they were doing along the way.

But because you've set your dream itself *without a deadline* you'll realize, when you regroup after a setback, that nothing that happens today can interfere with the operating plan. Your built-in revisions provide for unforeseen emergencies. Setbacks are *considerations,* not *impediments.* You'll be able to move slowly, firmly, and professionally toward that goal on the receding future horizon because nothing in the present can take it away from you. Before reacting strongly to each "No," you'll be able to tell yourself, "This doesn't matter in the long run, so what benefit can I turn it to?"

Does all this planning guarantee that you'll be "in control"? We know the truth about this one: No one's ever in control. But life is bearable when we grasp a sense of being in control; and having an operating plan to refer to allows us to set attainable goals, no matter how small, on a daily basis. Let's say that we're working on this particular objective because we have a goal, and see what results we can create in so doing. Then we'll correct our course of action depending on our observation of those results. As we move forward in this fashion, notice that what begins as a hypothesis often ends as a reality.

The important thing is to create a plan for your success that will allow you to keep the daily setbacks in perspective. Success experts agree that rejection and failure are the keys to success. All successful people have not only experienced rejection and failure, but have gotten good at it. "When I was a young man," George Bernard Shaw said, "I observed that nine out of ten things I did were failures. I didn't want to be a failure, so I did ten times more work." What separates the "successful" from those who haven't yet succeeded to the level of their goals is a fully detailed plan that allows you to visualize that success. What will you do when you've received that first check for $1,000,000? If you don't know, or find yourself resisting that visualization, you may be up against a self-sabotaging fear of success (identical with "fear of failure") that must be confronted and over-come. The operating plan details how you'll spend the money; how much you'll put away to give you the freedom you've been seeking, and how much you'll use to retire responsibilities. Some people reach the reward, then squander it all on debts and presents for themselves and friends, explaining the bumper sticker that reads, "Dear God, please let me make one more sale and I promise I won't piss it away!" The entrepreneur who's done this had learned to recognize the hard way that when the money comes the first priority must be using it to buy future freedom for further creative endeavor. If that means continuing to struggle to pay the weekly bills, then so be it. You've become good at that struggle, why give it up just because you have the money now? It's a truism that affluent people are sometimes the hardest to get to fork over their money, or to pay their bills. Maybe that's why they're affluent.

The plan begins, of course, with where you are right now. It should cover all areas of your life and activities: your health, your family, your social life, your financial status, your work accomplishments. While the operating plan should cover at least seven years into the future, I've written plans that have gone to age 90, just for the fun of it and to show myself how much time might be available. One thing the "long view" of time produces is an acknowledgement of just how much *can* be done in whatever space of time you decide you have left. Here's an example from a seven-year plan for a single mother in Kansas City moving, on a fast track (because she's dreamed about doing this for years) from being a nurse to fulfilling her dream of opening an antique store. Here's her situation:

- She's 30 pounds overweight.
- Her cholesterol is too high.
- She has $20,000 in her savings account when she sits down to write the plan.

- Her daughter is now seven, in school full-time.
- Nurses are in demand, and she can more or less choose her hours.

Her list of objectives, of course, will be revised and/or expanded at revision points along the way. She writes the first draft of her operating plan on August 1, 1994; and she'll revise and fine-tune it once a month, on the first of each month. During the first six months, she'll keep her day job; at that point, if all is on track, she'll move to nursing part-time, scheduling her hours around the needs of her antique store.

Operating Plan for a Career in Antiques

DREAM: To open my own antique store in Westport Landing, and travel the world purchasing furniture for resale.
GOAL: To earn a comfortable living selling antiques.

OBJECTIVES AND AGENDA:

- Research Continuing Ed courses on antiquing and business management (COMPLETE by September 10)
- Build a research library of directories and catalogs (ONGOING, but have the most important volumes on hand by October 15)
- Continue "antiquing" on weekends, talk to owners, auctioneers (ONGOING)
- Enroll in courses (COMPLETE by September 15)

- Complete both courses (COMPLETE by January 1, 1995)
- Construct budget in terms of needs and resources (ONGOING, but COMPLETE first draft by October 1, 1994)
- Locate affordable space to rent; close deal (ONGOING, but COMPLETE by January 30, 1995)
- Plan first trip abroad (ONGOING, but book tickets by January 30, 1995)
- On trip abroad, collect sufficient pieces to stock store (COMPLETE by February 28, 1995)
- Decorate the new store while awaiting shipment (COMPLETE by April 1, 1995)
- Plan opening day (APPROXIMATELY May 1, 1995)
- Plan next trip when income is sufficient to hire "store baby-sitter" (LATER)

She's decided this is as far as she needs to plan a detailed agenda in advance, but her operating plan will also chart her present view of what might happen in the six years following.

Of course she will alter her plan as she gains information. Her plan makes her Accountant slightly nervous because it only foresees six months in detail; but this woman has been listening to her nervous Accountant for years, and has finally realized that the Accountant is *always* going to be nervous. She's also figured out that if she continues working at least part-time and finds a place to rent for around $1,000 a month, her savings will carry her for at least a year.

AGENDA: (HPW = Hours per week)

By/ HPW	Personal Objectives	$ Objectives	Work Objectives
9/10/94 (10 HPW)	Weight to 120 Cholesterol 220 (exercising 3 hrs wkly/lo-fat diet)	Additional $2,000 to savings	Choose courses on antiquing/ business; continue antiquing
9/15/94 (15 HPW)		Do 2 hrs overtime to pay for housekeeper/ babysitter 7 extra hrs	Enroll in courses at Longview Community College; collect "library"; work on budget
10/1/94	Maintain 120 weight		Complete draft of budget; REVISE this AGENDA; RESEARCH TRIP abroad: choose region of France?
10/15/94	Cholesterol to 215		Assess library & plan on books to get, including guidebook to French towns & local papers
11/1/94	Weight to 118	Savings to $25,000	REVISE this AGENDA
12/1/94	Maintain 120 thru holidays (exercise 4 hrs weekly—1 hr can be walk)		REVISE AGENDA Start looking for space; TAKE 12/5–1/1 as VACATION from this operating plan

By/ HPW	Personal Objectives	$ Objectives	Work Objectives
1/1/95 (20 HPW)	Maintain 120	Savings at $23,000 Find "back up" investor in case store doesn't start paying for itself by 6/1/95	REVISE AGENDA (inserting detailed budget) Complete courses; BOOK TICKETS for trip
1/30/95			CLOSE DEAL on space in Westport
2/1/95	Weight to 115		REVISE AGENDA
2/28/95 (40 HPW)			COMPLETE TRIP
3/1/95 (20 HPW)	Cholesterol to 210		REVISE AGENDA Start decorating & naming store
4/1/95	+ 1 hr weekly swim		Set opening day; REVISE AGENDA; TAKE 1 WEEK VACATION to catch up with rest of life
5/1/95 (30 HPW)	Weight to 110		OPENING DAY REVISE AGENDA
6/1/95	Cholesterol to 205		Assess first month's performance; REVISE AGENDA

She hasn't projected what her income might be at the end of the first year because she knows she can't possibly predict that accurately. With her nursing to fall back on, she figures she can get by. And her goal is *not* to get rich antiquing; it's to earn a comfortable living antiquing. She knows enough about life to recognize that if she pours herself into her dream, she'll either get lucky or she won't. She has no control over luck, but she *can* control the time she devotes to the antique shop and the time she devotes to her day job.

The question her Mind's Eye brings into focus for her is, "Can I somehow make it through the next seven years if I know that by then I will be doing nothing but antiquing?" If the answer is "No," she needs to adjust the agenda, shorten the space between objectives, and/or find more time to work her new career. If the answer is "Yes," all she needs is to begin immediately—and to polish the plan monthly as she acquires more information about the new career.

The goal she's stated provides focus for creating an agenda by which specific *objectives* can be reached that will take her

Deadline	Health	Finances	Work
By 1/1/96	Cholesterol to 200 Weight to 105!	Store is "in profit"	2 trips aboard; part-time assistant
By 1/1/97	Cholesterol to 190 Maintain 105	Widen product line?	3 trips abroad; full-time assistant
By 1/1/98	Maintain	Look for larger store	4 trips abroad; QUIT NURSING!
By 1/1/99	Maintain	Into larger store; keep store #1?	If investor was needed, buy out investor?
By 1/1/00	Maintain	Store #2 in profit!	What do I dream of next?

inevitably toward the goal. She schedules time for revising her *goal*, and the agenda required to reach her goal through *objectives with deadlines*; and will therefore stay in charge of the process instead of letting the process take charge of her. She's decided at the outset that she'll take one day off every weekend to spend entirely with her daughter. Her agenda also includes leeway for sloughing off, and just relaxing— over the December holidays, and before the store opens. After all, she wants to treat herself like a human being, not an automaton mechanically unable to do anything except work. On the other hand, she may have scheduled fewer vacations than someone else in transition. As far as this woman is concerned, she's wasted too much time dreaming already—and needs to *act* on her dream.

Your objectives, revised as you learn more about your capabilities and as your luck changes, are the individual steps over which you have the greatest degree of control. After an internal trialogue among Accountant, Visionary, and Mind's Eye, you exercise your control by fulfilling a pact with yourself to put in the amount of time you've decided makes sense at that stage in the operating plan. In order to keep the Accountant from being overly threatened, this woman has decided to spend no more than 15 hours per week on the new career for the first few months, then to move modestly to more hours per week as she comes closer to operating her shop. If you take a gradual approach, and stick to your time-pact, you'll discover that the Accountant becomes your strongest ally once he's satisfied that this might all make sense and lead to something. He'll be knocking on your shop door, urging you to put in more time in this exciting new career.

What you've done is simply used all the parts of your

mind to translate your belief in yourself into an operating plan that allows you to bring your dream into focus, while also giving the dream the room it needs to grow and evolve.

Let me emphasize the revision aspect of the operating plan with the following observation of T.S. Eliot's: "The only method is to be very, very intelligent." Although operating plans are necessary as visualization aids, and as philosophical underpinnings, and as placebos for the Accountant, the truth is life itself has very little patience for rigid plans. The entrepreneur, by nature, will recognize and take advantage of unforeseen opportunities that have been generated by his decisive efforts in the direction of the dream. The career will evolve, and it would be a terrible mistake to prefer a preconceived plan to an exciting and immediate crossroads that involves leaving the plan behind or altering the dream. On her first trip to France, our new antique dealer runs into a French woman who wants to import American furniture. They work out an exchange whereby the French woman sends French furniture to the shop in Westport Landing, and the American woman sends American furniture to France—both of them marking up their goods for a sizeable profit. At this point, the original operating plan is subordinated to the new opportunity generated by the nurse's dream. She will postpone her desire to travel in order to fulfill her need (and her daughter's) for the "comfortable living." But the change fills her with exhilaration because it proves that fortune has smiled on her dream.

4

Stealing Time for Your Dream

Jack Smith: God created time so that everything wouldn't happen at once.

Atchity: Then how come everything keeps happening at once?

Accountant: You're living on borrowed time.

Mind's Eye: And since you don't have to pay time back, you can afford to enjoy it!

Follow your dream, and, by definition, you can't fail. Success lies in the following. If you have a dream, you have the responsibility to yourself and to the source of dreams to make it come true. That means finding time to "do what you have to do"—the very opposite of "marking time." Our minds experience life on a timeline of their own invention, a continuum that stretches from your first moment of consciousness to your last. "The end of the world," said Bernard Malamud, "will occur when I die. After that, it's everyone for himself." The human mind is like a time bomb, ticking away and trying to find time—until it finally explodes. And finding time in our accelerated world where we hear of "flextime," "time-elasticity," "the sweet spot in time," and "time slowing down" is more confusing than ever before. Years ago, if you missed a stagecoach you thought nothing of waiting a day or two for the next one to come along. Today you feel frustrated if you miss one section of a revolving door! So many of today's "time-saving devices" prove to be frauds—requiring more time to select, install, maintain, and update them than it used to take without them. It's hard to believe that a few short years ago we had not yet become addicted to fax machines, microwaves, VCRs, carphones, mobile phones—and even answering machines! All these inventions, as helpful as they can be to the Accountant's output level, suck up our time in ways that, unless they are examined and acknowledged, become quite destructive to the realization of the dream. More and more demands are being made on our time. Faith Popcorn (*The Popcorn Report*) puts its this way:

We're pleading to the big time clock in the sky: "Give me *fewer* choices, far fewer choices. Make my life easier. Help me make the most of my most valued commodity—the very minutes of my life.

It's time for the romance with Faster to come to an end, time to steal back the time that the gods of Fast have taken from us.

It's gotten so bad we can't really *manage* time any more. I think we're forced to *steal* it, invoking the assistance of Mircurius Caduceator, messenger, salesperson, trickster, and *thief* of the gods. Like any professional thief, Mercury insists on knowing as much as possible about the object of his theft and its natural habitat and characteristics before he goes into action. This chapter combines observations about the nature of time and work with practical suggestions about employing Mercury's caduceus to steal the time you need.

Bokonon: Busy, busy busy.

Ecclesiastes: Consider the ants. Yes, you are busy . . . What are you busy about?

Atchity: Does this mean I have to know what I'm doing all the time?

Our Puritanical upbringing has led the Accountant to want us to keep "busy." "Idle hands are the devil's workshop." One day I was consulting with an attorney who, by everyone's standards but his own, is quite successful. We were talking about forming a new marketing company. "Why do you want to do this?" I asked him.

"Because I want to get rich." He added: "I have to stop selling my time."

I nodded. "That's interesting." I was thinking of the reversible equation I'd written about in *A Writer's Time*: "time is money, money is time." "What brought you to this conclusion?" I asked him.

He told me that a self-made, wealthy, genius friend of his kept coming to California to visit. Each time, he'd say, "You're so smart—why aren't you rich?" The attorney had no answer for him, but the question continued to gnaw away at him.

Finally, on one visit, the friend had occasion to sit in the attorney's law office for an hour waiting for him to complete some phone calls. He had the opportunity to observe what was happening in the office.

On their way to lunch, his friend said: "You know that question I've been asking you all these years?"

"Yeah, of course I remember it—it drives me crazy. 'If I'm so smart, why aren't I rich?'"

"I know the answer now."

"Tell me."

"You're too busy to be rich."

Doing the wrong things, no matter how fast you do them or how many of them you do, will not advance your dream.

Those who break out of busy work and into the success they've dreamed of have learned to redefine time. If you recognize that time is merely a concept, a social or intellectual construct, you can make the clock of life your clock; and then determine what you do with it. More than the quantity of activities or completed projects I've managed to experience in my career transit, what I value most is the quality of time I've managed to steal from all those committees and examination-grading sessions. When someone asked me a few years ago to make a list of "things I do that I don't enjoy" I was happy to realize that it was difficult to think of anything other than my two to three hours per week of desk work that I don't thoroughly enjoy. I've managed to steal, for the most part, the right kind of time for *my* dream. Failure, for the Type C, comes in failing to steal the time you need to do what you dream.

What is time?

Unlike oxygen, an element which is objectively, scientifically definable, and more or less beyond our control, time is relative to perception and subject to choice. "Time," Melville wrote, "began with man." The Type C learns to redefine time "subjectively," in order to become successful by his own standards. Objective time, dictated by Greenwich Mean Time with an occasional correction for NASA, leads only to the conformity of repetition. Subjective time alone allows us to distinguish ourselves and to achieve our dreams of success.

Logos vs Mythos

The two primary ways of looking at the world in the time of the classical Greeks were known to them as *logos* (for the Accountant's logic) and *mythos* (for the Visionary's instanta-neousness). The Visionary's belief in eternity is what makes the Type C's life change from barely bearable to exciting. "To himself," Samuel Butler wrote, "everyone is immortal. He may know he is going to die, but he can never know that he is dead." The Visionary's eternity is the experience of *mythic time* that occurs when you "lose yourself" in the pursuit of your dream. It's Brer Rabbit's "briar patch" speech: "Throw me anywhere, but please don't throw me in the briar patch!" The briar patch is Brer Rabbit's favorite place in the world.

Sometimes you'll meet an old school chum after years and have the experience that "it seems like just yesterday" you were having this exact same argument, or laughing for the same reason known only to the two of you. A moment passes, as the Accountant wrests control from the Visionary: "But, on the other hand, it seems every bit like the 20 years it's actually been." *Has* it been 20 years, or *was* it just yesterday? Faulkner said: "There is no such thing as *was*; if *was* existed there would be no grief or sorrow." To the Visionary, time exists always in the present.

Accountant's time

To the Accountant, who's kept track of the years—and also the months, weeks, days, hours, minutes, and seconds—precisely, it's been *exactly* 20 years, and he can prove it by reciting all the events that have happened to both of you in the interim. The Accountant clocks time with digital precision, obsessive call-ins to the phone company's correct time service. The Accountant's time is what keeps society sane, if you call today's society sane. "Let's check our watches."

But when the Accountant's insistence dominates, you are denied making your dreams come true. The Accountant, nervous about anything intangible or "unseen," doesn't believe in dreams; or, at best, assumes the worst about them: "They're only dreams." Human beings can't fly.

Visionary time

To the Visionary, whose relationship with that same friend is/was intense, it's just yesterday. The Visionary clocks time only by reference to intensity. Lovers live from embrace to embrace, the time between "not counting." Have you ever felt like life would pass you by when you're stuck in an endless left-turn lane during rush hour? How long does a second last if you're perched at the parachute door of a plane at 15,000 feet about to make your first jump? How long is

40 seconds during a 6.6 earthquake? Or at the edge of a cliff, about to rappel for the first time?

The Visionary brings you mythic time when you engage in your career transit with all your heart, mind and soul, when you are occupied in doing something that "takes you out of time," or "takes you out of yourself." You're *ecstatic* which, from its Greek origins, literally means "standing outside" yourself. "I don't know where the time went" is what you say when you've just passed 14 hours creating a whole new multimedia, multilevel marketing plan—and your spouse, sent by the worried Accountant to tell you you've missed an important dinner party, is banging on the door because you've taken the phone off the hook. Like Alice's White Rabbit, the Accountant would always have you believe that you're late for a very important date. And the Accountant doesn't like it one bit when your Mind's Eye stops to question how important that date may be; or, whether you made the date in the first place or whether it was made for you. Type Cs insist on making their own dates because their Mind's Eyes have learned how to insure that mythic time gets preference over logical time.

You've had this experience: You've told yourself you're just going to steal "two hours" to work on your dream. You go into the briar patch. One hour and 55 minutes have gone by, during which you've been "lost"—fully engrossed in what you're doing, without a thought for the outside world that operates on the Greenwich clock. The hours have passed "like a minute" (the Visionary's way of talking makes the Accountant crazy). Then, you look up at the clock to discover that only five minutes remain of your bargained-for two hours. *How did you know to look up at the five-minute mark?* Because your Accountant never sleeps, even when he's been taken off duty. If you decide to remain in the mythic time of your dreamwork beyond the five minutes remaining—that is, beyond the two hours you set aside— the Visionary has won this particular encounter. The Accountant has lost. If you decide to quit "on time," you may think the Accountant has won, and the Visionary lost.

What's wrong with this win-lose scenario is that it's exhausting, and impossible to maintain in the long run. Most people, faced with this constant natural strife between the two aspects of their minds, have allowed the Accountant to take over entirely as the only peaceful alternative. They've chosen the Accountant's conservative, safe way of behaving because the daily battle is too costly in energy and emotion. If the Visionary "wins" the five-minute battle, for example, and you continue working on your marketing plan for another four hours instead of the two you'd set aside, guess how hard it's going to be for the Accountant to agree to the *next* two hours you want to steal. The Accountant will use every instrument in the arsenal of procrastination to postpone the marketing plan.

How to avoid losing time

Francesco Petrarch: It is appointed for us to lose the present in the expectation of the future.

Atchity: The present: lose it, or use it.

Petrarch, the first "Renaissance man," was aware that we spend a large majority of our time "somewhere else" than in the present moment. Planning for the future, worrying about the past—so much so that by the time you reach middle age the two horses, Past and Future, are engaged in a life-and-death race along your internal timeline. Competing for your vitality, stealing your present. The time you spend on past responsibilities, past regrets, past relationships, eats into the time available for growth and progress toward your future goals.

If we don't recognize "what's going on here," as Accountant time and Visionary time battle in our perceptions, we can get very confused. When we get confused, the Accountant can take control of our lives. For most people, the Accountant has been in full control. Consequently, they are frustrated, bored, caught in a rut. With the help of Mercury's powerful caduceus—whose two snakes represent, as in my dream, the taming of past and future around the strength of present awareness—the entrepreneur's now-open Mind's Eye can transform the bloody battlefield into the altar of your hopes and dreams. Awakening his Mind's Eye, Jack London said:

I shall not waste my days in trying to prolong them. I shall use my time.

This anti-Accountant declaration is made by your Mind's Eye who knows that only by marrying the Accountant's logic with the Visionary's myth will the present be captured for effective dreamwork—instead of the Visionary wasting the present in daydreaming, and the Accountant in obsessing. What happens when your Mind's Eye takes charge of the time wars is productivity combined with peace of mind. The photographer Ansel Adams said, "I'm amazed at how many people have emotional difficulties. I have none. If you keep busy, you have no time for them."

Work management doesn't work

Time and work are, in one essential regard, opposites.

* Time is *finite*. We only live so long and, while we're alive, we have only 24 hours in every day.
* Work is *infinite*. Work, whether good or bad, always generates more work, expanding to fill the time available.

Given this reality, it should be obvious that work is unmanageable; that only time can be managed. Yet people regularly sabotage themselves by trying to manage work. "First I'll catch up with my day job, then I'll take time for my dream," or, "First, I'll get my family in good shape, then I'll find time for myself."

Don't get me wrong. Work is what we're trying to find time for. Writers write. Craftsmen make tables or boats or flower arrangements. Actors go for auditions and interviews. Salespeople make sales calls—the more calls they make, the more sales. Shakespeare's "action is eloquence" is not only creatively productive, it's the best way to stay sane. Even one phone call a day in the service of your career transit, means, if you take two days off each week, 200 calls per year. That's definitely progress. Success comes inevitably on the heels of constant work, as the ancient Greek poet Hesiod pointed out in his almanac: "If you put a little upon a little, soon it will become a lot." Tom Bergin (Sterling Professor of

Romance Languages and Master of Timothy Dwight College at Yale) was the author of 59 books by the time he retired and 83 by the time he died. Yet he described himself as a "plodder." He just kept plodding away, in the vein of Hesiod. Tom and I managed to exchange hundreds of letters from the time I left Yale to the time he died. He taught me the relentless equation between consistent, minor actions and ultimate productivity. One day, by way of complaining about having no time to do any serious work because of all the trivial errands and duties he had to attend to, he sent me a quotation from Emerson: "Things are in the saddle and ride mankind."

Against the accelerating incoming bombardment of the *things* of contemporary life, Type C work happens only when we steal time to make it happen. Yet schedules, to-do lists, self-revising agendas are constantly being tested and found insufficient. They work for awhile, then fail. Without recognizing this reality, through the Mind's Eye's awareness, each failure may send us into a tailspin that moves us further away from success. Life insists on creeping in to sabotage our dreams. One of my clients, after six months of working together to change her habits to become more productive, told me I was the "Ulysses S. Grant of time management." She told me that Grant wired Lincoln: "I plan to hammer it out on this line if it takes all summer"—and that his telegram was read before it was handed to the beleaguered President. The jealous snoop told Lincoln, "You know, we have reports that General Grant drinks a considerable amount of whiskey." "Is that right?" Lincoln replied. "Find out what brand he drinks and send a case of it to each of my Generals." Lincoln recognized that whiskey was Grant's caduceus.

The human nature of time

Archimedes: Give me a lever and I can move the world.

Atchity: Time is all the leverage I need.

Using time as a collaborator begins with understanding its interactive characteristics and protean shapes. You'll begin noticing that time behaves differently under different circumstances. When you're concentrating, your awareness of time seems to disappear because you've taken yourself out of the Accountant's time and are dealing with the Visionary whose experience is timeless. When you're away from your career transit activities, you become very conscious of time because your Visionary is clamoring in his cage to be released from the constraints of logical time.

"You've got my full attention": compartments of time, time and energy, rotation, kinds of time, and linkage

Time-effectiveness is a direct function of attention span. When you're concentrating, giving the activity you're involved with your full attention, you produce excellent results. When your attention span wavers and fades, the results diminish. Until you recognize that attention span dictates effectiveness, you're likely to waste a great deal of time. The key to avoiding this situation is assessing how long your attention span is for each activity you engage in—and then do your best to engage in that activity in appropriate compartments, allotments of time that you've found most productive. Since my particular career is four-fold, I pursue what I call a "rotation method" of moving among activities that support my producing, writing, teaching, and consulting with my management clients. I love all these activities, but not when I do them exclusively—each one having its own high ratio of crazy-making aspects that automatically diminishes when it's juxtaposed with the others.

Except during a crisis is one of the four areas, at which point all other activities stand aside until the crisis is resolved, I find it stimulating to spend an hour working on teaching-related matters, then spending the next hour on calls that support various production projects in development. Moreover I've learned that it's a waste of time to try to control things that *only time* can accomplish—such as making a phone call, then waiting next to the phone for a response to it; or staring at the toaster waiting for the toast to pop up. The only time you have anything approaching direct control of anything is when the ball is in your court. So during that hour I focus on getting the ball out of my court into someone else's court so that the game can continue. Rotating from one activity to another insures that outreach begun in Activity A will be "taking its time" while I'm engaged in Activities B, C, and D. When the phone rings from the A call, I interrupt D to deal with it—and it's generally a pleasant interruption.

An hour happens to be my typical attention span compartment. But the length of the particular compartments ("compartments" are allotments of time given to a particular work activity) changes from time to time as my attention span for that activity evolves. During the drafting of his book, for example, I spent two hours a day writing, whereas before I began the draft my attention span allowed me to spend only an hour or less a day thinking about the book and gathering my notes for it. There's no magic formula for determining attention span because it changes as you and your circumstances change. Yet once determined, it is the mastering rod between the serpents, the compartment of time where past and future meet in a present that feeds from the first and nourishes the latter.

Obviously attention span is related to your energy level at different times of day, and with regard to different activities. Activities that drain you should not be scheduled one after the other, but should alternate with activities that create energy for you.

Energy and attention span will also be different depending on whether you are at the beginning, in the middle, or at the end of a particular objective. Your attention span is most in danger of sabotaging you in the middle, where it's easy to confuse your fatigue from the hard work of plodding forward with some sort of psychological upset with the process you're engaged in. Usually the solution to this situation is shortening the allotments of time you're devoting to the objective, or changing the activities around which you're scheduling this objective's compartments.

When a particular compartment is nearing a close, use the last few minutes of it (when the Accountant comes back online to remind you that the time is "almost up") to jot down what you're going to do in the next compartment. This automatically puts your Visionary and Accountant into a percolation mode in which they bat things back and forth "in the back of your mind" while you're busy working in the next activity's compartment.

Where does the time go?

The nonproductive Type C: "I don't know where the time goes."

Once your Mind's Eye takes over: "It doesn't go anywhere; time's in your face *all the time!* It's knowing what to do with it that counts."

For me, keeping track of time started at Rockhurst High School in Kansas City, where the Jesuits taught us to schedule our activities in precise Accountant segments. Here is what a page from the daily list I kept for four years looked like:

Note that the end of my March 1 daily agenda, which was written in pencil, was "tomorrow's to-do list." At 10:50 P.M. I allowed myself eight minutes to work on the next day's agenda. All day March 1 I'd been jotting down notes in pencil to remind me of things that had to be scheduled for March 2. During the eight minutes at the end of March 1, I created the agenda for March 2. Note also that all but one of the individual items on the March 1 agenda are items of "micro-management" (defined as *what* to do on the Accountant's clock *when*). The eight minutes at 10:50 P.M. are "macro-management"—considerably less than 1% of the time available to me.

Though it served me well as a foundation for future productivity, I'm sure it's immediately obvious that an adult living at the turn of the millennium can't live sanely for long with this excessively disciplined approach. But accurate description precedes effective prescription. For accurate consciousness of time-usage to arise, you must take control

Wednesday, March 1, 1961

5:30 - up; prayers
5:31 - teeth; face
5:35 - shave
5:40 - dress, hair
5:45 - room
5:50 - Ms, clox; basket
5:55 - reading
6:10 - paper
6:20 - M & C; Lee
7:00 - eat; clippings; read SM
7:30 - school; social; bull
7:40 - books
7:45 - office
8:00 - class
Study Hall
  Greek
  History
12:05 - Kali; schol?; deadlines;
  eat; social; office;
  read SM
1:00 - Study Hall
  Latin
  MM Mags
  Physics collate
           read bk.

2:40 - read
3:00 - AE
4:30 - home, mail; clippings;
  eat, social; papers, finances;
  exercise; Sat. work; library
MM, Eng., Lat; George; read
7:00 Reynolds
7:25 - services, mail
8:15 - read
8:30 - Broadmour
9:30 - read; feet
10:40 - record; chart
10:45 - teeth, face, dress
10:50 - schedule
10:58 - Exam C; AC
11:00 - TAPS

one way or another. As years passed, I learned I had to move on from the severe but satisfying monastic time-management methods of my Jesuit agendas. I experimented with macro-management techniques—what I call "the Gordian knot style of time management": Cut through the busyness by doing the important matters first, and letting everything else take care of itself.

The most familiar macro tool is the to-do list. It's excellent for getting specific small objectives accomplished, but ultimately you'll want to move on because using the to-do list to control your life ends up wasting too much time. Yes, you get the important little things done. But you can't write "become a shopping center czar" on your to-do list. The to-do list doesn't motivate or inspire you because it doesn't deal with goals and dreams, only objectives. That's why even the shortest to-do list often gets neglected, ignored, postponed, constantly "carried over" from one day to the next. Accomplishing it may satisfy your Accountant, but your Visionary is longing for more and feeling cheated.

I've developed two forms that can help you inventory your actual expenditure of time so that you can take charge of this most precious asset and attach it firmly to your dream plan—without becoming a Jesuit.

The Time Inventory Daily Work Sheet should be filled out at the end of each day, estimating the number of hours you spend on the various activities in your life. The example that follows belongs to an imaginary man who wants to move from his day job as a bank teller to being a self-employed independent insurance agent.

When you're filling out your own work sheet, don't forget housework, church and/or volunteer activities, phone time, etc. If the categories here don't sound right to you, alter them to suit your own life and activities. Don't add up the totals beneath or to the right until the week is over. But at the end of the week, add them up. Ninety percent of my students and clients end up with weekly audits far under or considerably over 168. What's magic about the number 168? The accountant is right about this one: 168 is exactly how many hours are inthe week for all of us—whether

Time Inventory Daily Work Sheet (in hours) Week of_____

Activity	Sun.	Mon.	Tues.	Wed.	Thur.	Fri.	Sat.	Total
Sleeping	8	8	6	7	9	8	10	56
Sales Calls	0	2	4	3	1	2	1	13
Exercise	1	1	2	0	0	1	1	6
Eating/Family	4	2	1	3	2	3	5	20
Reading	1	2	0	0	0	0	1	4
Hygiene	0.5	0.5	0.5	1	0.5	0.5	0.5	4
Proposals	1	2	2	2	1	4	1	13
Organizing	2	1	1	0	0	0	1	5
Driving-Errands	1	2	2	2	3	2	2	14
Socializing	5	1	2	1	4	5	8	26
Day Job	0	8	8	8	8	8	0	40
Total hours	23.5	29.5	28.5	27	28.5	33.5	30.5	201

you're the Pope, an ice skater, the President of the United States, a stock broker, a major league baseball player, a bank teller, or a hairdresser. The discrepancy between your count and 168 arises from your unawareness of the interaction among the three onboard voices in your mind. In his first week of keeping track, notice that our future insurance agent has recorded activities to fill 201 hours in the week. Where did the extra 33 hours come from? Now that he's admitted the discrepancy and recognized its magnitude, he's ready to get serious. Obviously he's more careful using the work sheet the second week, making sure he keeps closer tabs on where the time is going.

Once you've used these work sheets for two weeks, you have an accurate enough idea of where your time is going to make use of the Actual Time Inventory Analysis Work Sheet. Fill out the Activity and Hours per Week columns using the results of your second Time Inventory Daily Work Sheet. Now we want to find out, on a scale of 1 to 5 (5 being highest), how much each activity serves your dream goals. This is its Visionary Quotient. And we're not going to fool with "Sleeping" because the right amount of sleep is essential on all fronts.

There's nothing magic about filling out the Visionary Quotient column. Follow your gut reaction.

The Accountant's Quotient column rates the activity's importance to your physical, financial, and psychological welfare. Taking insurance classes, as far as your inboard Accountant's gut reaction is concerned, has minimal present value. Your pay check from the bank is keeping the potatoes on the table. Obviously, on the other hand, this man's Visionary hates his day job. But notice that neither the Visionary nor the Accountant is thrilled with the 12 hours

Time Inventory Daily Work Sheet (in hours) Week of:_____

Activity	Sun.	Mon.	Tues.	Wed.	Thur.	Fri.	Sat.	Total
Sleeping								
Total hours								

weekly this man spends on errands. Although some insurance agents might regard "socializing" as a valuable activity, our example obviously doesn't. His Visionary hates it as much as he hates his day job, and his Accountant rates it only a 2. If he's going to do anything about his socializing, he should think about socializing with different people (exchanging the coffee shop for the country club, where at least the social interaction might lead to prospects).

The third column, presided over by your Mind's Eye, combines the two quotients. This man's bank job is a pain in the neck to his Visionary, but it does pay the bills which the Accountant values to the utmost. It receives a 0 in the Visionary Quotient column, a 5 in the Accountant Quotient column. But your Mind's Eye acknowledges that any activity

Actual Time Inventory Analysis Work Sheet

Activity	Hours per Week	Visionary Quotient (1-5)	Accountant Quotient (1-5)	Mind's Eye Total (1-10)
1 Sleeping	56	xxxxxxxxxx	xxxxxxxxxxxxx	xxxxxxxx
2 Day Job	40	0	5	5
3 Eating/Family	14	2	3	5
4 Sales Calls	13	5	2	7
5 Insurance Classes	13	5	1	6
6 Exercise	6	5	3	8
7 Driving-Errands	12	1	1	2
8 Reading	2	3	1	4
9 Hygiene	2	1	2	3
10 Socializing	6	0	2	2
11 Organizing	4	4	0	4
Total Hours	168			

with a combined quotient of 5 or above will not be dropped or seriously reduced in time investment, thereby keeping both serpents happy.

The blank Actual Time Inventory Analysis Work Sheet below is for your reassessment. Fill in the categories to suit your own life.

Recognizing the unique power of both his Accountant's and his Visionary's perception of time, our insurance agent's Mind's Eye recognizes the *yin* of Accountant time and the *yang* of Visionary time as both valid, simultaneous, and equally important *in their places* and *for their purposes*. Telling them both that they're correct, and that they can take turns, his Mind's Eye negotiates with the Accountant to allow a conservative, cautious amount of time during which

Actual time Inventory Analysis Work Sheet

Activity	Hours per week	Visionary Quotient (1-5)	Accountant Quotient (1-5)	M.E. Total (1-10)
1 Sleeping		xxxxxxxxxx	xxxxxxxxxxxxx	xxxxxxxx
2				
3				
4				
5				
6				
7				
8				
9				
10				
11				
TOTAL HOURS	168			

the "success dreams" of the Visionary can be explored. Without the Mind's Eye's intervention, he was constantly conflicted over his use of time. With his Mind's Eye's help and negotiation, he begins to *steal time* for success, using his Goal Time Work Sheet to carve hours from the 24-hour clock and to mine, methodically, the breakthrough energy of the Visionary.

Activities that rate less than a 5 in the Mind's Eye column are subject to first-round negotiation. Let's say you hate doing yard work, and give it a 0 Visionary Quotient and a 1 Account Quotient. Obviously, we're going to find away to get that particular activity out of your life. In our insurance agent's inventory, "Driving-Errands" falls into this category. So he figures out a way of no longer doing errands. Instead of spending 12 hours a week on errands, he decides to do 4 hours of overtime at the bank to pay for someone to do the shuttle service for him. Or he moves closer to his day job. These revised decisions, which become "goals," are recorded in the Goal Time Work Sheet. Notice that by reducing "Driving-Errands" to 2 hours, and making a few other adjustments, he's been able to increase "Sales Calls" from 13 to 24 hours per week—which will inevitably advance his dream more quickly. At the same time, he's managed to increase the percentage of time devoted to the pursuit of his Type C dream from 16% (combining "Sales Calls," "Insurance Classes," and "Reading") to 26% because he's increased the time available to make those sales calls, but he's also changed his way of socializing so that it serves the dream as well.

No time you spend is more important than the time you spend scheduling your time; and that needn't be more than a tiny fraction of the time available to you. But scheduling your time is doomed to ineffectiveness unless you begin from the reality baseline of knowing what you've been doing with your time, and confronting your own lack of awareness about where your time has been going.

Goal Time Work Sheet

Activity	Hours per week
1 Sleeping	56
2 Day Job	44
3 Eating/Family	11
4 Sales Calls	24
5 Insurance Classes	13
6 Exercise	6
7 Driving-Errands	2
8 Reading	2
9 Hygiene	2
10 Socializing	6
11 Organizing	2
TOTAL HOURS	168

The blank Goal Time Work Sheet helps your Mind's Eye complete and memorialize its contract with Accountant and Visionary.

Once your knowledge of your time usage has allowed you to make new goals and objectives regarding the use of time, how in this busy, busy, busy world do you enforce the objectives for yourself? How can you schedule a life that is one, long, endless shrieking, demanding interruption? After all, you can only turn off the phone for so long without losing your illusion of control, and all contact with reality.

Goal Time Work Sheet

Activity	Hours per week
1 Sleeping	
2 New Career	Stopwatch hours:
3	
4	
5	
6	
7	
8	
9	
10	
11	
TOTAL HOURS	168

How to make "the clock of life" *your* clock: the stopwatch

Mercury's contemporary caduceus for taking command of your time is the stopwatch. Here's how you use this magic wand.

You know the clock on the wall will keep ticking away relentlessly until the day has gone by. You even know how it keeps ticking at night—why else would you awaken at 5:59 on your digital bedside clock when you've set the alarm to go off at 6:00? You know the telephone seems wired to that damned clock, life's interruptions seem wired to it, the myriad distractions that flesh is heir to seem wired to it—and you recognize that, as a result, you yourself and your dreams have been wired to the Accountant's clock for too long. Your world has been defined by that relentless uncreative clock. You are desperate to realize your Goal Time.

Today you stop the world. You buy a stopwatch. I suggest buying the simplest possible one you can find, one that allows you to stop the seconds and restart them, without the other countless 'modes' that will drive you crazy unless you're training race horses. Hang the stopwatch above your computer, your telephone, your work table—above whatever altar serves the god of your career transit dream. Promise yourself that, no matter what happens on that wall clock, you will work on your dream at least one hour before you go to bed tonight.

Or two hours. Try one first, then expand slowly and naturally in the direction of that Goal Time. Keep it as simple as you can and still make it work for you. Using the stopwatch allows me the illusion of freedom I value highly, but also the constant sense of disciplined progress toward the success I've mapped out for myself—nothing is more inevitable than the achievements that time creates in small, stolen increments. One hour a day is 30 hours a month. Thirty hours a month will inevitably produce results, especially if you've programmed the three parts of your mind effectively to make the best possible use of that one hour. Imagine how quickly our insurance agent will move forward, having assigned 24 hours a week to sales calls. He realizes that the faster he gets through those "Nos," the sooner he gets to the "Yes." And it just takes time to get through the "Nos."

If the one-hour-per-day approach doesn't work for your unpredictable schedule, or makes you feel too disciplined, make it a weekly approach. One of my workshop students was having trouble keeping to his contract that he'd put in two hours per day. After several give and takes, we came down to the real reason he was having problems: he was leaving his day job to be free, and the daily discipline made him feel enslaved. I asked him if he'd be comfortable committing to a weekly number of hours, to bringing in his stopwatch to the next session with ten hours on it.

"And I could do them in whatever configuration I choose?"

"Absolutely. The whole idea is to find a way of tricking your mind into allowing you to live by your own clock."

He came in the next week with 10:06 on his stopwatch, and the weeks after with 10:04, 9:56, 10:10. He'd found a way of using the caduceus to give him that necessary illusion of freedom and control combined with the satisfaction of real progress in committing hours to his career transit.

Crisis management

I wrote *A Writer's Time* when I was still a more or less "regular" professor, following a schedule that was generally set a year in advance. In the years since, the challenges to my time- and work-management needs and techniques became more and more unfamiliar. At the point when I had two films shooting simultaneously, two in preproduction, and four in postproduction, every morsel of time was a matter of what medical people call "triage." What do I do with this minute that will do the greatest good or the least damage to the overall project (my phone had five lines, *all* of which were lit up nearly 12 hours a day). How do you choose which call to answer when one is a director being interviewed, one a director in preproduction, one in production, and one in postproduction—and the other is the financer. How do you steal time to pull over to the curb and figure this one out?

When the first crisis occurred, I was convinced "we don't have time for crises." But that conviction soon disintegrated as crisis after crisis came along. Finally, I realized "we *have* to make time for crises." I asked my assistant to "time" the next crisis. Over a period of two weeks, we learned that an average of one crisis occurred each day, at unpredictable intervals; and, to my delight, that the average time for getting through the crisis and going on with our crazy "routine" was under an hour. Crises seem much more demanding to the Accountant's imagination; but by enlisting the Mind's Eye's help in timing them, the truth was revealed. The Accountant needs the help of the Mind's Eye to reduce crises to perspective proportion. Mercury's caduceus comes to his aid to realize that even crises can be managed by arranging to steal time for them. We began scheduling "throwaway" activities so that at least two of them were scheduled each day instead of being clumped into a "slow day." That way, when a crisis occurred, we could immediately implement the alternate plan for the throwaway activity. For example, I liked to be at wardrobe fittings for the leads; if a crisis occurred, I sent my assistant, with a Polaroid, instead.

Don't forget that only you can call "time-out!"

Anon: It's not over until the fat lady sings.

Atchity: It's not over, but I'm calling time-out.

I used to wish I could call "time-out!" on life, to give myself time to regroup and figure out "the meaning of life." I used to fantasize about building in an extra, dateless, hourless day each week to give us time off: no appointments, no phone calls, no deadlines. But that is daydreaming, undisciplined Visionary thinking trapped in an Accountant's world.

You can get time out on a regular basis—by stealing it. Now that you've embraced your career transit and are living the entrepreneurial life, don't forget to give yourself the benefits that your day job employer was forced to give you. Sometimes we are so excited about doing the things we love on a daily basis that we forget to give ourselves a break from them. "I don't need a vacation. My life is a vacation!"

Everyone needs vacations. Most people need them because work is exhausting. The entrepreneur needs them because vacations bring perspective and creative insights that are unavailable under the daily pressures of the career transit. "To do great work," says Samuel Butler, a person "must be very idle as well as very industrious." The entrepreneur, as both employer and employed, must schedule his vacations, with alternate dates in mind in case "something comes up" that forces a change. You are accomplishing just as much if not more when you "go away for the whistle" and allow your mind to play.

Vacations for the entrepreneur are excursions into Visionary time. "Getaway time," like the aboriginal "dreamtime," puts your Mind's Eye in direct touch with the Visionary's views of what you've been doing on a daily basis, and what you could be doing more creatively. Traveling away from "Base 1" is always good for the entrepreneur because it causes a "cross-pollinating" effect among your objectives, goals, and projects. But traveling must be distinguished from true vacations. Vacation is not going to New York on business, nor going home to see your family for a week. In both cases, there are too many things "to do" for the proper abandonment to occur. Vacation is being on the island of Maui, where, after a couple of days of readjustment to "heavenly Hana," your "to-do" list consists of two items, and you somehow never quite get around either to doing them or to caring that you didn't. You notice suddenly that the days seem long, immense; that time has become, as Jorge Luis Borges puts it, "like a plaza." Smaller getaways can produce the same effect: mountain hiking; wandering through the museum; deep-sea fishing for a day; just "hanging out" at Grand Central Station, watching the world go by. That is when Mercury brings you an Olympian perspective, where the patterns of your life and activities become apparent among the tangle of busyness.

It is precisely at such times that "chaos theory" applies itself to the entrepreneur's creative process. Chaos theory posits the all-important impact of tiny random events on the long-range prediction of physical cycles. Weather patterns could be predicted accurately were it not for "the butterfly effect": Somewhere a Monarch butterfly fluttering from flower to flower (an incident too small to measure) minutely disrupts the passage of the breeze, and a thousand miles away a middle-sized storm turns into a tornado. Chaos theory is the despair of Accountants, who spend their lives trying to predict regularity as though chaos didn't exist. But to the Visionary, chaos is the staff of Mercury. The German philosopher Friedrich Nietzsche, in *Thus Spake Zarathustra,* his most Visionary work, wrote: "One must still have chaos in one to give birth to a dancing star."

The entrepreneur arranges his vacations to put him in direct touch with chaos, following winding roads to heavenly dream places inaccessible to ordinary travelers.

Tips on time and work management

- *Rate everything that crosses your desk 1, 2, or 3.* Then make an agenda for the 1s immediately, and immediately delegate the 2s to someone else. Put the 3s in a drawer designated the "3 drawer," setting aside a few hours once a month to go through it and see what's still important enough to deal with. You'll discover that most of the contents of the 3 drawer are even less important then than they are now. Napoleon supposedly had all his mail dumped before the bags were opened, on the premise that the important news would have reached him already and anything he neglected that should not have been neglected would make itself known. I'm sure that Josephine quickly found an alternative method of communicating with her Emperor.
- *Postpone procrastination!* Anthony Robbins says, "The best way to deal with procrastination is to postpone it." Procrastinate with everything except your dream. To make that happen you need to—
- *As much as possible, solve each problem as it occurs.* Postponing the solution automatically increases the total amount of time needed to be devoted to it. Opening a letter, then stacking it somewhere, is counterproductive. If you know from the envelope that the letter isn't important, toss it in the nearest wastebasket and don't even take it into your den.

Selective pruning

Mencius: Men must be decided on what they will not do, and then they are able to act with vigor in what they ought to do.

Atchity: Don't do what you *can* do. Do what only *you* can do.

Just as the vitality of a tree can work against the tree unless an experienced arboriculturist is engaged to prune the weaker branches, dreams can be dangerous unless you understand their peculiar fertility. As work creates more work, one dream breeds another, usually grander than the one before. Success has ramifications, breeding all kinds of activities; and, unless you recognize that and infuse "regrouping" time into your success agenda, you'll suddenly find yourself "too busy" to be successful again.

Well-meaning Friend: You're such an enthusiast.

Atchity: Why does that sound like an accusation?

Enthusiasts must protect themselves from their enthusiasms. To accomplish this, I suggest the following.

• Hold a monthly "drop" meeting with yourself. The object of the meeting is to select activities that can be dropped for a month, with a promise to reevaluate their importance at your next meeting. I go through my project files monthly and force myself to table or discard the weaker ones, thereby constantly improving the quality of the projects I work on. As you become experienced in the Type C life, you'll recognize that one of its strangest characteristics is the necessity of killing the little monsters—that once were bright dreams—nipping at your heels. The smaller dreams must now be pruned away so that the bigger ones can thrive. Of course it's even better to kill them off before they begin, as Camus said: "It's better to resist at the beginning, than at the end."

- Don't feel bad about the discards. Celebrate them. More than sacrifices or disappointments, they are symptoms of your disciplined progress. Just because you *can* do something, after all, no longer means that you *must* or *should* do it. That was the old you, dominated by the Accountant, before your Mind's Eye opened to engage you in an entrepreneurial career transit.
- When evaluating new projects, keep in mind the sign that psychologist Karl Jung had framed above his desk:

Yes ~~**No**~~ ~~**Maybe**~~

"Maybe" is crossed out as well as "No" to remind us that it's the "Maybes" that devour our time and dream energies. If the answer to an incoming idea or request isn't definitively "Yes," it's definitively "No." Never Maybe. Maybe kills countless ambitions and splendid plans. "We are what we pretend to be," says Kurt Vonnegut's narrator in *Mother Night,* "so we must be careful about what we pretend to be."

You may also find it useful to go through the following checklist:

- *Is this a good idea (or opportunity)?* Yes or No.
- *Is this idea directly connected with my dream?* Yes or No. If

the answer is No, pass it along to someone else "with no strings attached."

- *Does this idea fit into my present agenda?* If not, is it such a good idea that I should revise my agenda to accommodate it?
- *Is the world ready for this idea?*

It's extremely important to consider both internal and external "timing" when it comes to evaluating new ideas and opportunities. Many of us waste time on good ideas whose time has either come and gone, or won't be coming for too long a time to make its present implementation productive. Of course, thanks to the predictably unpredictable impact of chaos on our lives, we can never be certain about timing. But we can be certain about our gut reaction to the checklist.

So long as you live, be radiant, and do not grieve at all. Life's span is short and time exacts the final reckoning.
—epitaph of Seikilos for his wife (100 B.C.)

5
A Day in the Entrepreneurial Life

Annie: The sun'll come out tomorrow!

Atchity: Meanwhile how do we make it through *today*?

One night, walking up to my front door, I realized that I was walking on air. I had experienced such a good day I felt I was living in paradise. I'd gotten up before dawn to write for three hours, closing on the ending of a new screenplay. Then I'd spent an hour exercising and reading a motivational book. After getting dressed, I went back to my desk and made phone calls—one of them to an agent who was thrilled to accept a client's novel for representation. At lunch, after discovering in the mail that one of my own books had been accepted for publication and a letter out of the blue from a professor who'd read my most recent essay and was inviting me to speak at Villanova and Bryn Mawr, I made a new financing contact, who assured me he'd get in touch with the man in charge of raising money for my next project. The afternoon had brought me the first meeting with an exciting new writing client, and agreement on casting with a finance company on a film about to go into preproduction. An early dinner with my best friend had been followed by the last meeting of my workshop where everyone thanked me for the past eight productive and happy sessions. Suddenly, I had a vision of an angry goddess coming around the corner and blasting me with a shotgun. And I realized I would have greeted death with a laugh. What better way to go, in such a great mood?

That was a good day.

The waiting room

Eliza: Just you wait, Henry Higgins, just you wait.

Atchity: I don't mind waiting if I have good work to do while I wait.

Most days are neither good, nor bad. They're a mixture, bringing as many moments of step-by-step progress as moments of new obstacles and aggravations. Getting through these ordinary days is the true test of stamina, because their endlessness is exhausting. I call these days "the waiting room," because so much of the time the career-transit hero is waiting for the new career to "take off."

At first, with your initial burst of energy, you try to turn the waiting room into the emergency room. Picking up the pressure, you think, will expedite the process. Sooner or later you'll learn that this approach produces diminishing returns. Most of the time, you simply have to wait. And waiting can be a real pain, though, as William Lynch reminds us, "The ability to wait is central to hope."

I've noticed over the years that I've formed what might be called a "waiting pattern," with the underlying theme of "work while you wait."

Breakfasting on hope

after Lewis Carroll: All the king's horses and all the king's men/Couldn't put Humpty together again.

Atchity: Never try to get your head together before you've found all the pieces.

My day begins by motivating myself to get out of bed in the morning. I've noticed that once I've actually got my feet on the floor, the day seems bearable. But dragging myself from the blankets can be a task that requires Mercury's guidance to accomplish. Those who embrace the dream quest know that the first important move of the morning is "getting your head together." You can do it in bed, you can do it while the coffee is brewing, or while you're having your cup of tea; some do it walking, jogging, or exercising. Others prefer meditation.

"Getting your head together," one way or the other, is a visualization technique: concentrating your inner vision on the potential positives of the day ahead so that you can turn to action which will inevitably, sooner or later, produce results. You'll decide how and when you'll focus today's ration of creative energy. If the day looks particularly forbidding, you'll decide how you'll protect that energy from the cruel world, remembering that you are its sole arbiter and protector. To fail to take the time in the morning to make those crucial decisions is to dishonor the dreamworld. Disraeli said: "We make our fortunes and call them fate." You must put yourself in charge of how you see the day ahead: "The fault, dear Brutus," as Shakespeare's Cassius points out, "is never in our stars, but in ourselves."

The entrepreneur's day begins properly when he has designed it to his own purposes. I can always tell how successfully my Mind's Eye is functioning by the length of time it takes me to rebuild my head in the morning. If I bound out of bed, it's because the dreamworld is so close to being a reality that even my Accountant can perceive it. If the process takes half an hour, I know my Mind's Eye had to work overtime to convince the grumbling Accountant and wounded Visionary that the good times will roll.

Mercury's inspiration means focusing on my *hopes* for the day, allowing the patron god of entrepreneurs to escort my weary soul into my chosen battle. I center my day in various ways depending on what I imagine it might bring. If the day's hope is that a decision might occur that I've been waiting for, or a check might arrive that's long overdue, I center myself by figuring out a way to protect that hope. If I'm supposed to call for the decision, I decide to call at 4 P.M., not at 9 A.M., so that I can have a good day in the meantime, either way. I also decide that, regardless of what I learn at 4, I will do something pleasurable at 5—take in a film, go for a walk with a friend, invite a favorite client or associate for a Cajun dinner. Planning for an enchanted evening always gives me something to look forward to. Now I can make it through anything.

If I see no hope at all on the day's horizon, I do my best to manufacture some. For me, this means taking all the phones off the hook to spend the day writing, with my back to the world. I've noticed that doing this generally produces two benefits: first, I feel great about myself after a day of solid creative endeavor; and second, the world seems to feel bad about being such a deterrent to my dream and almost always has something hopeful to report the moment I switch it back "online."

At the worst extreme, I force myself to leave the house and go off for a cup of coffee in a public place. I remind myself that the world I live in is the world I've chosen for myself and designed. It doesn't take long, when I compare my situation to what I imagine to be the situations of the passersby I observe, for my psychic energies to regenerate. I recognize that I prefer my lifestyle to that of the non-weird. I also remind myself that it's not necessary to see a happy conclusion to my whole life—it's enough simply to visualize making it through the day with my hope and vision intact. Creative intensity demands that as much as possible I remain intent in and on the present. I remind myself that focusing on my work, whatever happens, will leave less time for worry. Some people recommend smiling at yourself in the bathroom mirror. I recommend singing in the shower. I used to have a sign posted inside the medicine cabinet: "Yesterday hero: today superhero." The sign was to psyche me up for the battles of the day by reminding me that I'd heroically overcome those of yesterday. It gave me something to sing about.

Good Morning: vision and salesmanship

The best morning is one in which you accomplish another step forward toward your goal from the height of your enthusiasm. I schedule *new* sales calls for the morning, or working on my latest writing project. What these activities have in common is that they are more, rather than less, under my control, whereas actions that are already part of a project in progress are already tied up with forces beyond my control. A typical morning is getting up at 6 to hit my writing desk by 6:30. I write until 8 or 8:30, then begin making marketing calls, first to New York (before they go to lunch), then elsewhere. As much as possible, I try to follow up immediately after each call. If someone wants to see a screenplay or a book, I write the cover letter and arrange to get it on its way before going to the next call.

This is "prime outreach time." Because I've noticed that my belief in myself is always strongest at the moment of initial contact with a new associate, I *initiate* in the morning, putting my belief into action. Give yourself a limited number of high-priority *new* sales calls to make each day and you will see your action produce results. Worst case, you will be getting through that finite list of "Nos" as quickly as possible—not forgetting to turn each of them into a future "Yes."

When you believe in yourself and/or your project, your vision becomes contagious, assuming you either have, or can fake, the self-confidence required to follow through. Success comes from making other people see what you see. From ancient times it was a seer or a prophet who sold society on what it should value most highly. Your objective on each sales call is to create the lens through which the prospect views what you're selling. Never allow "cold readings." If you can't create a positive lens, focus on creating a neutral one by seeking an open-minded consideration.

Keep in mind, no matter how pressured you are emotionally or financially, a long-term relationship with your buyer is more valuable to your dream than an immediate sale. (Your buyer is not responsible for your present needs, much less for your past problems.) The "right network" for you will be one of mutual respect; where your buyer respects your product even if it doesn't fit his needs at the moment, and you respect your buyer's needs. Never or at least rarely try to sell something to him that doesn't fit his market. Listen to your prospect. Pull back the moment you sense a negative decision, and begin working on the future of the relationship.

I've discovered that a sales call works best for me when I couch it as an information call. I'm calling to inform someone about a product, and to ask their advice on its market; and to inform myself about the market, as seen through the eyes of this particular buyer. Couching a call this way *always* allows me to enjoy it, and to make it a positive, hopeful experience.

No one can reject you but yourself!

Anon: A prophet is rejected in his own country.

Atchity: Reject rejection!

Of course you can't avoid hearing the word "No." If it's true that you can't fail at being yourself, why does that word hurt so much of the time? Because you're just not good at it yet. You've got to fall in love with "No," learning to see it as a come-on, an enticement, a challenge. One way or another, you must deal with "No" to suit your own purposes, looking for the chink in its armor.

Some writers burn their rejection slips. Others have more scatological approaches—like the German composer, who wrote to a critic: "I am sitting in the smallest room in my house. I have your criticism in front of me. Soon it will be behind me." At the outset of my free-lance writing, I papered the bathroom wall with the worst of my rejection slips. My father came to California for a visit. I hadn't told him about the guest bathroom. When he went to use it in the middle of a dinner party, he returned to the table with a long face. "What's wrong, Dad?" I asked.

"That bathroom," he said. "I'm really proud of you."

Then, after a few minutes had passed, he added: "God, that's depressing." I learned more about my father's conservative nature that night. He didn't like to be rejected, and had constructed a life for himself where little rejection could occur. I didn't like rejection either, but was trying to master it. At first by blatant confrontation, but gradually by redefining all these "Nos" as steps forward.

Whatever your approach, coming to terms with rejection is an absolutely inevitable early stage of success. Thomas Edison said, "He who's never made a mistake has never made anything." The sooner you're rejected, the sooner you'll be accepted. Think about it. If what you're proposing *weren't* original and unique, everyone would say "Yes" immediately. You're doing something new, so rejection is predictable. After all, if they're telling you "No!," they're the wrong people for you. Do you want the wrong person to say "Yes"? Enormous time can be wasted when the wrong people say "Yes." You need not only a "Yes," but a "Yes" from the right person.

As you get into rejection, you learn to transform each "No" into a "linkage." Each conversation that is less than a definite "Yes" becomes a definite "Maybe" because you accept the buyer's needs and because you don't associate his present, temporary "rejection" of your product with a judgment about *you*.

Don't be quick to conclude that a negative response is a rejection. Keep in mind that everyone is saddled with "lack of self-confidence," including your buyer. A negative initial response can often be turned around by your insistence, with all due respect, that the buyer doesn't understand the value of the product you're offering and you'd like a chance to demonstrate it to him. Often your excitement, when you believe in it enough to press it, will open the buyer's mind to seeing the product your way.

Even if you've had a dozen negative responses in a row, and you're beginning to think all the odds are against you, don't let your current discouragement turn into pessimism. Optimism is still the only policy that makes sense. The truly great salespeople base their success not on what they've sold but on the act of selling. They love it! Even after they've made millions, they can't stay away from that door behind which another "Yes," or a challenging "No," or a definite "Maybe," may lurk.

Doing lunch

In my business, lunches are so traditional that it took me years to realize that they aren't necessary much of the time. New York is so much more practical in this regard. A typical introductory meeting in New York begins with 5 or 10 minutes (max!) of small talk, then gets down to "what can we do for each other," and ends in 30 to 45 minutes. After several such meetings, if the parties are *simpatico*, a lunch or drink might be in order (though rarely necessary). In Los Angeles, the pattern is the opposite, no doubt caused by the city's magnificent geographical challenges. Getting together is an occasion. A meeting can consist of 45 minutes to an hour of small talk, usually surrounding diet, health, and relationships; and the final 15 to 30 minutes is reserved for exchanging business objectives.

I've discovered that I prefer the New York pattern, but that many others in Los Angeles prefer it also. I've also discovered that few people are offended if I try to conduct the same business, or even the get-acquainted conversation, over the telephone, which is an enormous time-savings. I've reduced my business lunches, from an average of four a week in Los Angeles, to one or two a week. I've also learned to replace lunch with a shared walk. I schedule my management and consulting clients between 12 and 3 because I know everyone else in town is at lunch during those hours. Or I'll schedule a late-afternoon "drink" instead of lunch, so that I can spend the lunch hour on the phone with New York (before they leave for the day), or catching up with my desk or reading motivational or instructional literature (with the side benefit of not ruining my diet from too much restaurant food). The point is always to create your day around your purposes, finding new ways to advance your dream.

"How softly runs the afternoon"

The afternoon, for me, is a time to wind down and to lessen stress. After making an hour's worth of follow-up calls after lunch, I try to find an activity associated with quiet to take me to dinner time. This is a great time for errands, for catching a film, for reading, for going for a drive, taking a walk, or taking a nap. From 3 to 4 I'm on the phone, from 4 to 5 I try to find that quiet time. When I do, I find that the hours of 5 to 7 are highly productive—usually receiving phone calls from people who've waited until the end of the day to deal with a project. So from 5 to 7 I schedule activities at my desk that can bear interrupting (letter writing, accounting, organizing, making notes on tomorrow's marketing calls). I'm happy to be interrupted by the phone.

Enchanted evening

Cajun proverb: There's always something to celebrate.

Atchity: Celebrate making it through the day.

You're not going to have a terrible day if you've planned a pleasurable evening. That's why planning the evening is one of the most effective methods of centering yourself in the morning. Make the evening a time to celebrate, to retreat, to play tennis, to make love, to pretend, to hang out with friends and family, to enjoy the fact that you're alive, to abandon the hunt, taking your daily vacation from the intensity of your life. I have to fight myself away from the desk sometimes in order to put this into practice, and I don't always succeed because my desk is usually overflowing, and I love the work I do. But I find fun in the evening most consistently when things aren't going as smoothly as I'd like them to during the day. If the evening has been enchanted, your dreams will be sweet dreams—the best possible preparation for a bright tomorrow.

6
Dealing with Money

Jack Benny: I never said money was the most important thing in life. . . . It's just a heck of a long ways ahead of whatever's in second place.

Accountant: You're living beyond your means.

Visionary: Then get your ass in gear, and increase our means.

Cajun Saying: You know you're still alive if it's costing you money.

Time and money form the lifeblood of dream. Yet we live in a society where, according to some, it's more painful to speak personally about money than about sex. Our Accountant is especially strong because of the Puritan heritage bred into most Americans, our national love affair with practicality and immediate security.

Tom Bergin used to write to me encouragingly, "Don't worry about money. Money always comes." I used to find it exceedingly difficult to relate to this advice, thanks to my accountant father and money-conscious family. But I've found it's true. Somehow there always seems to be enough for what's important. You will find a way to "access" what's required, as another mentor, Linda Levinson, once told me.

Money *does* grow on trees. The money tree is the fertile, well-managed garden of your mind. Someone once told me, "You think money comes out of a faucet, endlessly," and I replied: "It does." Consider Walt Disney's attitude toward money:

I've always been bored with making money. . . . I've wanted to do things, I wanted to build things. Get something *going*. People look at me in different ways. Some of them say, 'The guy has no regard for money.' That is not true. I *have* had regard for money. But I'm not like some people who worship money as something you've got to have piled up in a big pile somewhere. I've only thought of money in one way, and that is to do something with it, you see? I don't think there is a thing that I own that I will ever get the benefit of, except through doing things with it.

Herb Goldberg and Robert T. Lewis, in their fascinating book *Money Madness*, offer a corollary: "When the satisfaction in *having* money submerges the satisfaction derived from the *process of making* money—then it can be said that the person has an unhealthy attachment to money."

Early in my career change I visited the father of one of my Occidental College students, a semi-retired Prussian immigrant who had done well in "the new country" as a manufacturer. I'll never forget what he told me about America. "There's no reason," he said, "to fear failure in this country. There's no penalty for failure." When I asked him what he meant, he explained bankruptcy to me.

Growing up I'd heard the word on more than one occasion. My father had undergone a severe mid-life crisis of his own after the Pabst Blue Ribbon distributor for which he'd worked for 25 years suddenly went bankrupt. But before that I'd always heard the word in reference to my grandfather Atchity (we called him "Jede"). Jede, an immigrant from the "old country" of Lebanon, had gone bankrupt in America more than once. When World War II broke out, he'd just opened a candy factory and ordered a trainload of sugar for which he'd agree to pay 22 cents a pound. By the time the train pulled into Kansas City, the price of sugar had fallen to 15 cents a pound. He'd also gone bankrupt when he invented a sanitary napkin he called Motex, and was undercut by Johnson & Johnson, who came out with Kotex priced "two for the price of one" until Jede's company bit the dust. Yet by the time my grandfather died, he had amassed a sizeable estate, enough to be proud of—especially considering that he'd raised a family of seven. I remember him as an energetic man, who knew how to relax with his music and laughter, but who, like my mother, always urged me to "go for it." He was the one who supported me when I decided, standing in the freshman registration line at Georgetown, to register for classics instead of pre-med. My father had a hard time with the phone call I waited three weeks before making. "What are you going to do for a *living*?" he said. But Jede was proud of my decision and never doubted that I would someday become a "distinguished professor."

Society had not penalized him for failing. It had encouraged him to succeed, by allowing him to survive financial catastrophes through bankruptcy. Yes, you may have trouble with credit. But entrepreneurs always find a way; and "money talks." You can have zero credit and, when you have sufficient cash for a substantial downpayment, buy whatever you need or want to buy—on "time."

Success is failing forward as quickly as possible. It's a

question of perspective, and what you're willing to sacrifice, and how you choose to see yourself.

At one point three years into the career change, after Lorimar Home Video went bankrupt, I was left in a disastrous financial position—suddenly overextended, and personally at risk. The prospects of income, overnight, were reduced from a minimum of $250,000 per year to a minimum of zero. With only three years' business experience, and having spent most of my time in Montreal for the duration of the films' production, I had made no provisions for this Los Angeles corporation's bankruptcy. As I returned to Los Angeles and struggled to keep my production company from drowning, I was to face personal bankruptcy every single week for the next six years. I had to sell my company, L/A House, because the money it was owed by distributors was so far in the future as to be irrelevant to my present. I had mistakenly associated my dream with L/A House, and had put all my eggs into its one basket. With the help of my best friend and of my trusted legal adviser I recognized that the dream wasn't dead. It was still alive, although wounded and whimpering, within me. They taught me to associate the dream only with my own identity "so that flags, if necessary, can be left behind on the battlefield" and the war can continue. At the same time I was going through the psychologically painful transition in loyalties, I was struggling to learn the television business— where cash flow, until it's extraordinary, is laughable.

In the midst of my struggles, my father was diagnosed with cancer and given six months to live. He fought the diagnosis bravely and lived another two years so that he, an Accountant to the end, could make sure he'd put all his affairs in order. At one point, when I was visiting him in

Kansas City, he gave me the blessing a son sometimes waits a lifetime for in vain. He told me I had always been a good son, and that he knew I'd achieve what I wanted to achieve; but that, in the meantime, I should declare personal bankruptcy and "go on with" my life.

His words lifted an immense burden from my shoulders. Not that I declared bankruptcy—I managed to hold it off, through some of the "hooks and crooks" described below. But I *gave myself permission* to use a perfectly legal, and increasingly acceptable instrument of American society—if I had no alternative. Before I had assumed I would be in disgrace, with society and especially with my father, if I repeated *his* father's pattern. But my father had always been a fair man, and he was judging fairly that I had made my best efforts to recover and should not continue making efforts that were counterproductive to my future potential.

Living on the edge

Accountant: You like living on the edge, don't you?

Atchity: Yes—and it's okay to admit it.

I was telling a friend in New York that the "edge" is always wider than you imagined. He disagreed. "It's narrower than you imagine," he said. "But the longer you live on it, the wider it can get. At ten years, you can widen it yourself."

My widening formula goes this way: I will do everything short of bankruptcy to keep afloat, including negotiating with bank creditors for extensions in payments, etc. I realized that my crisis was *their* crisis as well, and that they had a stake in my recovery which I might use as leverage when I needed it. And if they did *not* cooperate, I would offer them the alternative of my bankruptcy.

I discovered, as I put this plan into action, that living on the edge was a much wider existence than I'd previously imagined. I had seen paydays, the 1st and 15th of the months (and I hated those short months where they came closer together), basically as "the end of the world." Bad attitude! I have since learned to see them as turning points and challenges, and feel an immense satisfaction after I send out all the checks that I can afford to send out and shuffle the papers in the "1st" or "15th" files to hold over until the next period.

But when I wasn't able to make the institutional payments on the assigned date, I learned that nothing life-threatening happens. Of course I always knew that. Everyone's overlooked a payment and received a gentle reminder. In fact, we receive these gentle computer reminders sometimes even when we don't overlook a payment, with their last line: "If you have already sent payment, please disregard this notice." It's important to fully assimilate the fact that these reminders come from computers. If you are having that nasty personal involvement with your self-image and lack of funds on a given day, it may help you to focus on the fact that it's not an angry father or an angry god who's slapping your hands. It's a coolly efficient, temperature-controlled computer. No human beings involved.

Yet. Humans do get involved later. But when they do, their focus is entirely on collecting the money. Inquiring about your plans to pay it. "When can we expect a payment?" They negotiate, they listen, they give advice. They only get angry when you ignore them. Not to experience all the stages of the process is to deprive yourself of an invaluable course in business reality. As someone who'd dutifully paid everything on time through years of my academic career, I was living in a magic kingdom with an unreal view of the actual edge and my degree of freedom.

Now, thanks to my challenging difficulties, I know I have much more maneuvering room than I'd thought. This gives me greater self-confidence. No one wants me to declare bankruptcy, but the only person holding a gun to my head had been myself.

"Do what you love"

People are divided into those who go to work to earn a living and those whose work earns a living for them. The first group, accounting for approximately 95% of the human race, is security conscious, trapped, perennially bored and in need of entertainment. The second group, the Type Cs, have exchanged boredom for terror but having found their vocation find the strength to deal with terror. And, given the choice, would cling to their present terror rather than return to the security of boredom.

In the midst of the crisis to my first company, I asked myself a hundred times a week if I'd made a terrible mistake leaving the serenity, respectability, and security of Occidental College. It got so I couldn't tell which onboard voice was asking the question, the anxious Accountant, the crazy Visionary, or the disappointed and ready-to-concede-defeat Mind's Eye. After one particularly painful day, one of my beleaguered entrepreneur friends had tried to explain to me how much he valued his weekends at Army Reserve camp where he got to wear a uniform that everyone automatically respected instead of walking around naked in the jungle. I realized I, too, missed the uniform. It was so comforting to belong to a social group where I received automatic respect.

Once, I drove to the Occidental campus around midnight and sat on a bench in the Spanish neoclassical quad, surrounded by Oxy's famous roses. It was a strange experience, a kind of agony in the rose garden, for the first few moments as I breathed in all I had given up. But I hadn't been sitting there for more than five minutes when the familiarity of my former life swept over me. The sensation was unmistakable: it was the very feeling of *suffocation,* including the sense of being left behind by the "real world," that had led me to make the exit decision in the first place. It had taken me nearly a year, after receiving tenure, to identify that feeling. But I recognized it immediately when it returned to me that night.

As I drove home, feeling much better now that the voices were sorted out (the Accountant had been the culprit, as might have been predicted), I realized that I'd just tested for myself what my best friend had been telling me consistently: "You made the right decision." He'd also added: "Don't be a baby. You've been spoiled as a professor, and now you're in the real world with the big boys." On the drive home I recalled the feeling of flying through the blizzard from Montreal to Toronto where I wasn't the least bit worried about the zero visibility and turbulence because I knew that if I died then I'd be dying in the middle of my own dream. I was doing what I love to do. Leonardo da Vinci put it this way: "As a well-spent day brings happy sleep, so life well used brings happy death."

My grandfather had always said to me, "Do what you love to do. Don't worry about the money." I advise my undergraduate and graduate students, as well as my clients, "Find something that makes you happiest, then figure out how to make a living doing it." When I was happy teaching, I couldn't *believe* people were paying me to do what I would have done free. To be paid to do dreamwork is what we're all aiming for. My son, back from Salamanca for a visit, told me at lunch one day that he'd figured out, remembering my advice, that "being in Spain" made him happiest so he'd decided to move to Madrid and find a job where he could get paid for loving Spain and being fluent in Spanish language and culture. An excellent plan.

The comfort horizon

My goal has been a comfort horizon of three years, allowing me more time for purely creative efforts. My objective is a comfort horizon of six months, which will allow me to 'catch my breath." I've frequently achieved the objective, but the nice thing about it is that it requires constant reachievement. After six years of such achievements I've begun to experience a new level of self-confidence. I don't have to reduce my expenditures to make the paydays. I've chosen instead to maintain and increase my income. The struggle has helped me to discover new resources within myself. Through it all, I've discovered that I *can* make it in the "real world." My worst year financially has been 30% better than my best year in my former career. My best year has been ten times better.

What about rainy days?

Dad: You need to save for a rainy day.

Atchity: It never rains in Southern California.

Looking back on my decision to move to Los Angeles after completing my graduate work at Yale, I don't remember my father being a vital factor in my taking up residence in a city where it rarely rains. But now I wonder. Growing up in his house in Kansas City meant listening to the distilled wisdom by which he ruled his life, one of his favorites being the necessity of saving "for a rainy day."

I remember subjecting that statement to intense analysis at one point when I wanted to use nearly all my savings to buy a new car. A "rainy day," by his definition, was a day in which a sudden emergency required an immediate infusion of cash. He himself, like his father before him, had experienced more than one such rainy day—and, unlike his father, had survived because he had prudently saved money. (My grandfather had survived by his wits.) What were the possible rainy days in my life? I was fully insured medically, and also had life insurance (both of which I've made certain to maintain, at my own expense, through the career transit). My auto insurance covered accidents and injuries. I couldn't think of any other rainy day worth worrying about. So I put my father's proverb aside.

It's extremely important to re-examine the proverbs you inherited, and to replace them with your own. What does "a penny saved is a penny earned" mean? I thought it meant it's not worth saving a penny because a penny will never be (much) more than a penny.

Jugglers and tightrope artists

Beckett: Do not come down the ladder. I have just taken it away.

Atchity: Which leaves me in a precarious position.

The successful high-wire acrobat does not look down. The dividing line between success and failure is a single misstep; proceeding with a dangerous self-chosen career risks that failure at every turn. You can't be a juggler if you're not willing to drop the ball. You learn to improve *only* by dropping them. A tightrope artist must be willing to fall, as much as he concentrates on avoiding it. Jung puts it this way: "Where there is a fear of falling, the only solution is to jump." Think of all the money that you've spent so far as part of our investment in yourself. The time to analyze the risk-reward ratio is when you've struck it rich. It's impossible to analyze it before that moment because you don't yet know the final numbers. Looking back at the money you've spent is something you can do from the luxury of the mountaintop. Looking back before you've reached that point just makes you dizzy and interferes with your climb.

Safety nets and catastrophe scenarios

Tightrope artists begin with a net. They become fully familiar with the net before they climb to the wire, testing its strength, bouncing up and down on it to convince themselves. They attempt new tricks only with that safety net beneath them.

I discovered that a "catastrophe scenario" created such a safety net for me. If I could *not* make it through one of the paydays, I went from Condition Green to Condition Yellow, following Donald Trump's advice: "If you plan for the worst—if you can live with the worst—the good will always take care of itself."

- During Condition Green, where the comfort horizon was a minimum of two months (meaning that I could clearly see sources of income that would take me through all the paydays in the next two months), I dedicated my daily schedule to long-range, high-income projects like writing new screenplays or reading books that I might option or creating business plans to raise production financing. But when an unexpected event caused the comfort horizon to shrink drastically (a deal falls through, someone who owes money suddenly goes "belly up," a distributor's check bounces), Condition Yellow has begun.
- In Condition Yellow, I have to concentrate on alternatives for the short-range, cutting back on all long-range activities except those that require a response from me rather than an initiation.
- Condition Red cuts in when Condition Yellow activities seem fruitless. Because of the recent recession we've all been blessed with, Condition Red has occurred more than once. Condition Red requires focusing on examining, maintaining, and mending the safety net. The safety net might include:

—looking for a job;

—moving to a less expensive abode;

—declaring bankruptcy (including knowing the telephone number for the attorney, knowing what to do first, knowing who to pay and who not to pay);

—warning people you are contemplating bankruptcy; and

—regrouping after the battle has been lost so that the war can continue.

I've gotten so good at repairing the net that I've never had to use it. Something about focusing a day's activity on these fail-safe plans seems to prod fate to get back in your corner. Note the important omission from the Condition Red catastrophe scenario: giving up the career *is not* an option. Selling popcorn at Disneyland or waiting tables is the rule rather than the exception for people in the entertainment business who have not yet made their mark. Each time I've constructed the catastrophe scenario I've felt better because I've realized that although I might suffer untold pain in the short run, nothing that happens to me in business can stop me from achieving my dream in the long run. It also helps to have read about the careers of other entrepreneurs in my field. They've nearly all gone through hell to get to their goals.

Short run vs long run

Obviously the entrepreneur engaged in career transit finds himself constantly alternating between short-run necessities and long-run desires. How do you know how much energy to invest in each? How do you decide whether a detour is, instead, an entirely new route?

I try to focus on the short run only to the extent necessary to make the long run possible. Sometimes this principle makes no purely financial sense. For example, you need $10,000 a month to keep your chin above water. Following the Cajun proverb, "If you can touch bottom, you ain't swimmin' yet!" you are treading water month to month with $9,000 to $11,000, robbing Peter to pay Paul, juggling, tightrope walking, etc. And your present comfort horizon is maybe two months. Note, too, that seeing is believing. It's not money that motivates the entrepreneur, it's hope. When your Mind's Eye is convinced it sees future income, your motivation level remains high despite the Accountant's recognition that future income is not actual income until it materializes. Accountants are trained to see only what's in front of their noses right now. From the unrelenting daily struggle, sometimes your Accountant's glasses need cleaning.

In the midst of the struggle, someone comes along and makes you "an offer you can't refuse." My own career quest hasn't been faultless in this regard. It was two years after I'd produced the 16 films and the heroic path had taken a disastrous detour with the bankruptcy of Lorimar Home Video and my consequent inability to retain control of my first production company, L/A House. A financer offered to pay me $15,000 monthly, indefinitely, plus shares in his company, if I would use my marketing talents to sell *orange juice* for him in Montreal, Toronto, Paris, London, Madrid, and Rome. "What about my brilliant career in show business?" I asked. "No problem," he replied. "You can do that on the side."

I soon found myself suddenly far away from the center of filmmaking, making what was for me an unbelievably good living selling fresh orange juice in Europe as the vice president and marketing director of a company whose name I'd invented. For a few months of first-class travel I was proud of myself because, according to what I read in a *USA Today* report on American salaries, I was making more than the governor of any state in the United States.

I learned the hard way that this is an offer you *can* refuse if you keep your goals in mind. Although I *can* market orange juice, it's not something only *I* can do. In my dreams I didn't *need* to market orange juice, and suddenly woke up at the Lord Byron Hotel in Rome one morning realizing how off-track I'd gotten—because I was worried about the flight home the next day, even through it was first class. Then, as if to underline the revelation it was intent on making, my unconscious managed to lose my glasses in Antigua. Realizing that I wasn't being fair to my own career ambitions or to the orange juice czar, I resigned from *Freshhh!*.

I'm willing to call this decision to quit *Freshhh!* courage, though I credit it more to my learned ability to listen to my unconscious mind and the signals it regularly sends me than to any virtue of consciousness. The familiar sensation of suffocation alerts me that all is not well.

The entrepreneur's goal is not to make money, but to earn his living doing something he loves to do.

Fresh orange juice may have been challenging, but it's not my lifetime love.

When I walked away from orangeing Europe, despite the fun of staying at the best hotels in those wonderfully romantic capitals, I knew in my gut I was doing the right thing. My faithful assistant Jane Singer, who had suffered through the detour with me, congratulated me on the decision even though we both knew it probably meant the end of our working relationship. But she told me, "This is the best decision you've made in a long time." I'd gotten back on track, by renouncing the temptation of money. I won't tell you how my father reacted to this news.

The detour reconfirms the route. Although I falter now and then, I've learned to no longer question the shape of the career I've chosen to pursue. I've "gotten my act together." All other considerations are secondary to that, though I've learned that the process of being yourself is first and foremost a *process*. Knowing yourself is the most challenging education of all, the final frontier. And nothing teaches you more about yourself than making a career transit in a world in love with pigeonholes and niches.

Money and self-esteem

Porgy: I got plenty of nothing, and nothing's plenty for me.

Atchity: If the choice is between wealth and dreams, I choose dreams.

Most Americans, I would venture to guess, connect their self-esteem with how much money they have—either in their pockets or in the bank or in "receivables." Career transit has taught me to count money in my pocket rather than in the bank or in the future as sufficient for my present mood. My unconscious, as always, was way ahead of me on this. I remember the day I realized that every time I took money from the ATM I automatically began humming the song about "a pocket full of beans, a new pair of jeans." The physical act of putting money in my pocket gave me enough confidence for the day.

It's easy to talk positively when you're feeling positively, but when the prospects for getting through payday without going to Condition Red are dim, often you're not feeling so positively at all. That's okay. Go away, as they say, "for the whistle." Take whatever time you need to work through your dark feelings because you *must* work through them one way or another before your head is clear enough to figure out new solutions to the present crisis. I discovered by watching my behavior over the years that the worst of times are those weekends that fall before a 1st or 15th during a Condition Yellow. I used to spend the weekends in intense anxiety because there was little I could do on the weekend to solve the problem that I imagined would plop itself squarely on my face on Monday morning. After years of this behavior, burning out a number of wonderful Zuma Beach and Central Park companions along the way, my Mind's Eye realized several things.

- The Monday Morning Problem was never as urgent as I imagined it to be.
- Whatever happened on Monday morning happened regardless of how I felt over the weekend.
- Every time I went through the down-cycle depression of these weekends I emerged with solutions that allowed me to deal with the Monday Morning Problem.

From these observations my Mind's Eye concluded that my life would be more pleasant if I decided, on Friday, that I would limit the anxiety to part of the weekend instead of all of it, and would make sure I spent that anxious part either alone or with a best friend who would provide perspective. I've even managed to achieve some Condition Yellow weekends with no anxiety, by getting down to listing the solutions on Friday rather than waiting to go through the soul-searching that led to writing them down Sunday evening.

It's okay to give anxiety license, as long as you managed it by compartmentalizing in this fashion. Once you give it license, the anxiety isn't nearly as interested in laying you low as it was when you allowed yourself to be tortured by it.

Part of the intensity of these weekends' anxiety was how I felt about myself when things "looked bad" financially for Monday morning. I had to work through feeling like a failure, work against the image of my father worrying, so many years ago, about how I was going to "earn a living." My self-esteem was still tied up with money, no matter how few beans had to be in my pocket to get that song going. I'm not sure you can ever completely overcome this childhood hard-wiring. But having your Mind's Eye become aware of it is a tremendous step toward managing it on a daily basis.

The wolf at the door

Well-meaning Friend: How are things going?

Atchity: *Where* things are going is all that concerns me.

One of the reasons I prefer business to being "an academic" (as in a cocktail party exchange I overheard recently: "Are you academic, too?" a professor asked the woman I was with. "No," she replied. "I take iron.") is that businesspeople aren't afraid to use clichés that portray life more vividly than precisely invented original language.

"How are things going?" I'd ask a fellow entrepreneur.

"We're about to go belly up," he replies, shaking his head.

I could tell by the way he carried himself that "going belly up" was not necessarily the end of the world. The metaphor gave him detachment. Using the language of the "game" brings perspective. As long as you realize it's a game, you're still in charge.

If you don't, the clichés can kill you. You've got to learn to master them.

"What would you do," a student in a weekend career transit workshop in Minneapolis asked me, "if you end up face down on the pavement in a pool of blood?"

"How deep is the blood?" I wanted to know. If it's not too deep, and I haven't drowned in it, and I can't walk because "they" came and broke my legs, then the answer is: "Crawl forward."

The cliché that used to concern me the most, as I explained to Dr. Joyce Brothers, was "the wolf at the door." I finally learned that dealing with the wolf at the door begins with walking to the door, having your Mind's Eye do a "reality check," then talk to your Accountant about its choice of vocabulary. If there is no *actual* wolf at the *actual* door, you're okay. The wolf is a product of your imagination (terrified Visionary and nay-saying Accountant conspiring to frighten you) and your imagination can be tamed by your Mind's Eye.

Examine the financial metaphors that the clichés of

family, friends, and associates inflict upon you and make them your own.

They: He doesn't have a pot to piss in.

Mind's Eye: Thank God that's true. I have a modern flush toilet that's infinitely preferable.

They: He spends money like it's going out of style.

Mind's Eye: But it's not, so there's no problem.

They: You're robbing Peter to pay Paul.

Mind's Eye: Exactly. Then I rob Paul to pay Peter. So it all works out.

They: What will you do if a rainy day comes?

Mind's Eye: Rejoice We *need* rain in Southern California.

As Humpty Dumpty told Alice, "Words mean what I want them to mean." It's a question of who's to be the master, we or they.

I used to imagine, returning to Los Angeles from a business trip where all had not worked out as positively as I'd hoped that "the guys" would meet my plane at Los Angeles International and lead me away in handcuffs ("the guys" being American Express, MasterCard, VISA, and Discover). It hasn't happened yet, though the metaphor still entertains my debarkations from time to time. That's simply not how it works in this country.

Burning bridges and striking tents

Career transit candidates want to know, "When do I burn my bridges?"

Burning bridges means cutting yourself off from your former career so that you're forced to deal with your new career with all your energies. I burned my bridges when I was in production with the first eight Lorimar films by resigning from Occidental College. Before that moment, I had been shuttling back and forth across the career bridge like Stonewall Jackson's Army of Virginia—fighting the battles on both sides—by taking first one, then a second, year leave of absence. But the decision to take a leave of absence without pay came as a result of very specific symptoms. I had gotten to the point in my new career where the "development" of my film projects was becoming intense; I was wanted on the phone constantly. Meanwhile, I would be sitting in my office at the college conferring with students about their concerns. The phone would ring, interrupting the conference. When this began to happen regularly, I realized clearly that my two careers had reached the conflict point. I wasn't being fair to either by trying to shuttle the bridge.

Only you can define your conflict point, and sometimes you can't define it in advance. You'll simply recognize it when it arrives. In general, you burn your bridges when you're forced to choose between one shore and the other. And, of course, you choose in favor of the new career.

But don't burn your bridges before you feel you either have to, or can afford to. I burned mine only when I attained a comfort horizon of two years. One of my clients announced to me six months into his first novel that he was thinking of taking early retirement in order to devote full-time to his writing. His family wasn't thrilled with the prospect, but after asking him about his retirement income I encouraged him to move forward. He was using the opportunity to test my belief in him, and I had zero doubts about his talent. He's now retired, finishing out his last year of "work," and happily halfway through his third novel.

Redefining financial security

Obviously my client got to this point by redefining his needs for financial security. If he was now making $4,000 monthly, and living comfortably, but unhappily because he had so little time to write, how could he feel making $3,000 monthly, living with more caution, but having an additional minimum of eight hours per day to write? Even his family came around when he helped them visualize the change in his temperament.

The self-esteem that begins to creep in when you've firmly decided to go for it will bring you the strength to deal forthrightly and creatively with bills, creditors, and the issues around money in general.

Invest in yourself!

It never ceases to amaze me that people who claim to be making a career transit hesitate about investing money to expedite that transit. One side of them has their priorities straight, the other is trying to sabotage them. One of my workshop students recently asked me if she could pay the workshop fee in installments. She started to rattle off all the expenses she was experiencing with her business and her family, when I interrupted her. "Of course you can partially defer the fee, if you really need to. Do you really need to? Think about it, and what kind of statement you're making to yourself." She continued with her list, then paused. "I'll call you back," she said.

When she called back, she was elated. She'd had a long discussion with her husband, who told her she should be investing in her new career. "So I want to pay the whole fee upfront," she added. My question had made her stop and think, and get her head together. She recognized that the Accountant was using lists of expenses as a means of telling her she wasn't worthy of a career transition luxury.

In situations like this, people also somehow forget their business common sense that tells them that any new business *requires* investment of money as well as of thought, time, and energy; and will profit from the experience of experts. People who resist the investment are indulging in magic thinking, and would rather waste years on wild goose chases than avail themselves of shortcuts. The money you spend with books, workshops, and consultants—if you've selected them carefully through common sense questions and reference-checking—may save you ten times as much as you'd spend learning on your own. By definition, second careers are more time-sensitive than first ones, where, in the expansiveness of youth, we think nothing of making the same mistake over and over again.

Anything or anybody who can help you move more quickly toward your dream career is a proper investment. Refusing to make such investments may be your Accountant's way of sabotaging this very "threatening" career transit. The money you spend is "only money"; the time you waste is the only time you have.

Creative money management

When things are going well financially and there's plenty of money, of course you'll pay everything on time—sometimes ahead of time, to know that your comfort horizon has been secured. But when things are rough, here are some hints for dealing with your career transit finances gleaned from my experiences along the way.

Reduce your overhead

Every dollar that goes to overhead takes away from the longevity of your career transit. Toughing it in the short-range insures your long-range success. Besides, toughing it is romantic: candlelight at home, instead of at the posh restaurant; eating lobster at home instead of out; renting two videos and turning off the phone instead of spending money on an evening at the cinema.

You don't have to pay all your bills on time.

Ideally, you might say, it would be nice to be *early* in paying (you receive a large check, and pay your rent three months in advance). If that is an expression of your creativity, do it. Otherwise realize that not even your Accountant wants you to be early. When I can, I pay early just to remind myself who's master. If you're late, of course, you pay penalties— but so what? I've overheard people talk about how much they hate to pay late charges. "How much was the late charge?" I'd asked. "Sixteen dollars!" they reply, "but it's the principle of the thing." Well, if you're working a secure job, then that very well may be an exciting principle to you. For the entrepreneur, the principle of the thing is paying when you can pay. You don't mind being "penalized" when you can't pay because penalties are part of the game. How good a hockey player would you be if you were so worried about the penalty box that you never got close to the opposing players? Pay when you can, and don't worry about it.

You don't have to pay everything that's "due" each time.

Pay something. Pay what you can. Pay what you feel like paying. In the long run, only nonpayment destroys your credit. Imperfect credit is so normal it's not worth worrying about if you've already chosen the path of the Type C.

Your credit rating is not all-important!

But your dream is, and the dream, when it arrives, will overshadow the credit rating. Credit ratings aren't cut in stone, either. If you have the skills to succeed at the level of your dreams, you'll have the skills to get what you want with or without a perfect credit rating.

Improvise.

There are many ways to keep the computers out there happy. Happy computers are busy computers. One entrepreneur told me that when his receivables didn't show in time to make his payments, he put pinholes in all his checks so that the computers would kick them back. Then he replaced them, one by one, as the receivables trickled in. I'm not recommending this procedure, but I am recommending

that you apply your entrepreneurial creativity to the Accountants' world that keeps bringing those paydays around
with such relentless regularity.

Juggle money every two weeks, not every day.

You can obsess about your financial problems daily, even
hourly, but that's giving money an awful lot of control over
your life. You acquire a definite illusion of control if you
postpone major obsessing sessions to the 1st and 15th of the
month.

Write your checks "on time," send them out on your time.

It gives me the illusion of control to know that the checks
are waiting to go out as soon as the universe cooperates and
provides sufficient balance to send them. Even when I have
money, now, I send only one check out at a time—choosing
to control the outflow.

Rob Peter to pay Paul.

Having several accounts helps. Of course you may run out
of juggling room at some point, but that's what Condition
Yellow is all about.

Make them beg.

Dad, I know this sounds terrible, but why should I be in
such a hurry to pay every bill exactly when it's due?
Obviously you should do so when you have plenty of
money available, and you do so when the debt is owned to

an individual whose personal finances are affected by it. But in those dry spells when you don't have plenty of cash available, hold off paying the others as long as you can. I've known affluent people who pay their bills only when the pressure becomes extreme. At first, I found this behavior hard to reconcile with their possession of so much money. Now I wonder if it explains why they remain wealthy. They aren't in a hurry to pay up. At the very least, don't be in such a hurry.

The check is in the mail.

How many times have people told *you* that? Why aren't you using the same tool once in awhile?

Taking advantage of the obvious.

MasterCard and VISA have funded a goodly number of career changes. Once my drycleaner, who'd arrived in Beverly Hills from Iran less than a year before, looked worried when he made his weekly drop-off, and I asked him way. He told me he'd opened up a second shop.

"Already?" I said. "Business must be great."

"It could be better. I used MasterCard," he told me. He'd been issued a credit line and used it to the max. A year later, he'd opened up his third shop. That's the spirit. Having survived life under the Shah and the Ayatollah he figured, "What's the worst that can happen to me in America?"

Use your own creativity to take control of money.

Most Type Cs have at best an ambivalent relationship with money. I remember once telling a therapist that I felt bad for crumpling up my bills in my pocket instead of folding them neatly in my money clip. I knew my father would disapprove. "How much money would you estimate you've lost in your lifetime because you wad your bills up?" she asked.

I gave it some thought. "A few dollars maybe," I said.

She'd made her point. Wadded money was just as effective as folded money, but with one significant difference. It made me feel better to crumple it. Money is the means to an end, not the end in itself.

For a long time I made a practice of depositing in a savings account all checks I received with odd cents in the total ($5.61, $281.43, etc.). I didn't like all the rules I'd grown up with about how to save money, so I invented one that I could call my own. Once, when Roy Disney told his brother Walt that the bank was adamant about their catching up on a $20,000,000 loan on which several installments had been missed, Walt told Roy that he planned to solve the problem by asking them for an additional $20,000,000. Roy hit the ceiling, demanding how Walt could even think they'd agree under the circumstances. Walt was puzzled by Roy's response. "What choice do they have?" Walt asked him.

Gamble only on your self-investment.

Of course play the lottery from time to time, but don't invest more than a few minutes in gambling at the slots or the crap table or the stock market. Early in my career transit, my then-wife discovered a stock for us to invest in. I agreed to contribute part of the investment, then changed my mind. The more I thought about it, the less sense it made. I knew my career change would involve all my powers and resources, and more money than I could foresee. I explained to her that I couldn't feel right investing in anything other than what I was going for. Stock market investment is a crapshoot over which the investor has zero control. I have a good deal of control over the pursuit of my dream. Your best asset is yourself, and therefore you must be your best investment.

Expect to invest money in your career, as well as time and energy.

Businesspeople expect that new investments cost money. Take a businesslike approach, but evaluate each expenditure cautiously, doing your best to make sure that the money is being well-spent.

Use the resources around you.

When the wolves are howling around the answering machine, and you've done all you can to fend them off on your own, consult one of the many services available to help you manage your creditors. That's where the Accountants shine. Don't forget to use them. You'll learn much about the resiliency built in to the American system.

Don't be afraid of the IRS.

Keep records. As an entrepreneur, you're more likely to be audited than you were as an inhabitant of a secure day job. It's not because they hate entrepreneurs, it's because they understand the pressures entrepreneurs are under and want to make sure the pressures don't lead to tax evasion. Ever since my father taught me to type tax returns for his clients when I was six, I'd regarded the IRS as the fiercest dragon in my hero's journey. But, having come through a three-year audit recently with flying colors, I'm delighted to report that my inboard Accountant's insistence on record-keeping tamed the dragon. Yes, they did ask for records. Yes, I spent a number of miserable hours preparing them. Yes, they asked for explanations and an account of my business activities. But, working through my C.P.A., I satisfied them. I had taken business deductions aggressively, and all my deductions were, in the end, accepted. In fact, at audit's end, the inspector told my C.P.A. that everyone should take deductions aggressively.

Throughout the process I felt increasing self-confidence. What had begun with fear of the unknown was turning into a familiar battle, in which my job was to bring ammunition and weapons from my arsenal to bear against the enemy and to continue bombarding them with my resources. I'm good at that. And the battle was won.

When I have money, everybody has money.

Rick McKeown, my entrepreneur brother-in-law, is the first one I heard in my adult life stating what I now know is the universal catechism of all those who don't have a "regular cash flow." But growing up the statement came out, as a negative, from my father like this: "With him, it's either feast or famine." It's taken me all my life to realize I don't mind the feast-or-famine scenario. I happen to love feasts, and don't mind fasting. If the alternative is a "sensible three meals a day" every day, I'm with Rick. Don't let the metaphors grind you down.

Seriously, how bad would it be to get a job, or keep your present job?

An actress explained to me that she'd managed to earn a good living for the first three years of her new career, but that this year had been tough and she was about to go back to waitressing (which she'd done before her first "gig"). "That's great," I congratulated her. She looked surprised, then realized that I understood. It's great that she so easily can slip into a day job as undemanding of psychological resources and as flexible with schedules, and as easy to leave behind the moment a major role announces itself. Don't let your "pride" stand in the way of taking care of business and doing what has to be done. Your pride should be invested entirely in the ultimate fulfillment of your dream, and what must be done along the way is only a means to that end.

"When prosperity comes, do not use all of it."

I believe Confucius said this, and it's worth listening to. Once your dream begins to generate income, you will experience the sweet sensation of being compensated for being yourself. If you're good at it, the compensation may suddenly increase dramatically. You may "strike it rich"! When that happens, don't forget your highest value is the freedom to continue pursuing your dreams. Buy more of that freedom by retaining some of the abundance you've earned. You see how my father's "rainy day" philosophy has evolved.

7
Dealing with Your
Mind/Body Asset-Base

Motto of Jesuit order: *Mens sana, in corpore sano.* (A sound mind, in a sound body).

Atchity: Surely you jest.

Arab saying: On the day of victory no one is tired.

U ntil then, it's normal to be exhausted. Once you get by the *madness* of making a career transit, and have constructed an operating plan, all focus must be on *methods* for implementation. Only method counters exhaustion. The reconstruction of your own positive reinforcement on a daily, sometimes hourly, basis requires an operating plan that's firmly tied to your dream—and consistent discipline to move forward despite all obstacles or considerations. At the same time you must become more adept at avoiding negative reinforcement of all kinds: symbolic, personal, psychological, family, and physical. You must also short-circuit the need for immediate reinforcement if you wish to accomplish something grander than anything you've previously accomplished. As much as I enjoyed writing them, I stopped doing book reviews regularly for *The Los Angeles Times* when I committed to my career change. The reviews gave me immediate rewards but drained energy and time from the long-range dream.

Physical health

Press: Why did we invade Granada, Mr. President?

Reagan: Because nutmeg comes from Granada. No Granada, no nutmeg. No nutmeg—no Christmas!

Atchity: No health, no energy—no dream.

During my first career, my efforts to maintain a sound body were sporadic, at best. But the career transit has forced me into health. I can't afford "sick days" because *I'm* the business; and without my healthy activity level things don't move forward rapidly enough to satisfy me. In the last five years I've exchanged aspirin, blood pressure medication, antibiotics, and prescription sleeping pills for Chinese herbs that maintain all the foibles of my system without the side-effects. I use the treadmill at least three times weekly, and try to play tennis or to walk the other four days. Fighting with my weight is a constant struggle, but I make progress by more or less maintaining a low-fat diet. I get a regular massage once a week, and a deep-tissue massage at least every other week. I pursue every lead I hear that promises greater health because I need my energy level.

I used to feel a little odd about this gentle fanaticism, even though I live in Los Angeles, the health fanatic capital of the terrestrial universe. (We'll admit there may be healthier beings in other galaxies.) But then one of my clients invited me to join him at a nearby health spa for an evening of sauna, steam room, and hot and cold springs. On the way I asked him how often he visited the spa. He said he tried to make it once a week, but at least every other week.

"You do more body stuff, and more head stuff, than anyone I know," I remarked. He had just turned me on to "blue-green algae," as well as to an herbalist.

"That's right. I do everything I can think of. Gotta take care of my chief asset."

Which is exactly the point. Luxuriate in taking care of yourself. Now that you've "gone for it," and committed to following your dream, you owe it to yourself to take care of yourself. Regard all health-improvement expenditures as priorities, and don't defer them "until you make it big." One hour of exercise in the morning is probably worth two extra hours of sleep—explaining why one of my ICM agent-friends gets up at 5 to spend two hours at the gym before work.

I rarely lose a night's sleep, despite the stressful lifestyle I've chosen because I promised myself, at the start of my career transit, that losing sleep over this new career was a symptom of not being able to handle it. Take your sleep very seriously. The minimum you require for functioning with a clear and rested brain is an unnegotiable need. But make sure you've done everything you can to make your sleep restful. To begin with, unless you're allergic to cotton, buy an all-cotton mattress with an all-cotton cover that breathes through the night instead of emitting noxious fumes. Engage only in soothing activities before falling asleep (sex is best during the day). I don't watch television before falling asleep because it fills my head with incoming stimuli at a time when all I care about is shutting down the onboard computer so it can reshuffle and sort its programs. Instead I find reading a half page of almost anything instantly knocks me out, no matter how charged-up I felt before I began reading.

If you're going all out in your rush toward the wall gate, you will still get tired. But you'll know enough about yourself to recognize the difference between physical or psychological fatigue and "depression." My herbalist tells me that since I use my brain so much I have to take herbs to cool it and calm it down. I used to think he was nuts, but I tried it. Metagenics TCB3 (a combination of various herbs) does, in fact, calm your brain down. I rarely get headaches, and generally sleep soundly.

Even on the day before victory fatigue may be a constant companion dogging your heels. Don't confuse your exhaustion with anything other than its physical reality. It is not a psychological warning that you've moved to the far side of madness; nor is fatigue emotional despair that you've overreached your limits; and it is especially not a mystical command to go to work for the post office. You guard against fatigue through foreknowledge of your own system, when you care to apply it, and through regular physical exercise and frequent vacations.

Emotions, mood, and attitude

F.D.R.: The only thing we have to fear is fear itself.

Atchity: No wonder we have our hands full.

The most important success in an entrepreneur's life is his present mood. "The way things are going," as Robert L.

Kuhn noted, "is more important than the way things are." I've found it useful, at various turning points in my career transit, to keep track of my mood on a scale of 1 to 5 (5 being best)—jotting today's rating on my day-runner page or in my journal. Somehow the simple act of recording betters the mood.

- 5—Complete optimism. Things couldn't be going better. I'm looking at the Promised Land.
- 4—Things are going great. I can see the light at the end of the tunnel.
- 3—What happened? We're in a "stall".
- 2—I've faced worse than this.
- 1—How are we going to get out of this one? Time to mend the safety net.
- 0—Condition Red. Total despair.

Usually after a few days of recording, you'll find you no longer need this little trick because the "mood rating" scale brings internal perspective. Compare today's crisis to ones you've weathered before, and remind yourself that you've already faced this challenge and dealt with it successfully. Remind yourself that you've faced more complex crises than today's. And that, with any luck, you will someday face more complex ones than you can even imagine now. Remind yourself that your mood has been lower. Finally, when your mood sinks to 1 or hovers near 0, remind yourself that you're about to turn a corner because it's always darkest before the dawn.

One particularly stressful day my phone mania was interrupted by the doorbell ringing. It was the plumber, come to fix the toilet. I directed him toward the bathroom, and went back to the unruly phones. In the middle of my next conference call I realized I was having difficulty hearing because of the noise level coming from the bathroom. When I hung up, I followed the sound of singing, becoming less annoyed and more interested the closer I got to its source. He was on his knees, working on the toilet, singing at the top of his lungs.

"Are you always this cheerful?" I finally asked.

"You bet I am," he said.

"Why?"

"Because it's my attitude. All I got is my attitude."

"Your attitude?"

"They can take my job away. I can go home and find they've taken my old lady away. They can even take my home away, but they can't take away my attitude!"

The psychologist Viktor E. Frankl must have encountered the same plumber. Frankl says that the last great human freedom is the freedom to determine your own attitude. Once attitude is determined for the positive, the next step is protecting it and therefore protecting the energy that positive attitude brings to daily life.

Perspective and self-investment

Karl Menninger: Attitudes are more important than facts.

Atchity: Minute by minute, my attitude is my greatest achievement.

The Visionary is generally so intense and concentrated that he loses sight of the woods for the trees. The present crisis is the end of the world. Today's problems are the worst ever. Perspective is therefore the most crucial helpmate your Mind's Eye can provide. Perspective comes in two varieties: perspective toward yourself, and perspective toward others.

When people are dying in ethnic conflagrations and from starvation all over the world, how upset am I allowed to get over a financer not returning my call for two days? "External perspective" derives from the ancient observation that there isn't a shred of evidence in human history suggesting that life should be taken seriously. Of course the Accountant takes life seriously, which is why he's often anxious; but that's why he needs to be finessed. But the Visionary takes his Vision with equal seriousness, which is why he's often terrified. Your Mind's Eye takes your work, not yourself, seriously. Donald Trump, in *The Art of the Deal*, puts it this way:

One of the keys to thinking big is total focus. I think of it almost as a controlled neurosis, which is a quality I've noticed in many highly successful entrepreneurs. They're obsessive, they're driven, they're single-minded and sometimes they're almost maniacal, but it's all channeled into their work.

Taking your vision seriously is distinguished from the futile rigors of self-involvement. Self-involvement is narcissism in isolation, leading nowhere, with nothing to offer outside yourself. Self-*investment* is self-involvement turned toward action in the public arena. When you are self-invested, you do the best you can and leave the rest up to the Fate who watches over the efforts of entrepreneurs.

High anxiety: "Can't live with it, can't dream without it."

Every entrepreneur I know wishes that, until he's learned more about his nature, he could reduce the anxiety level of career transit. Yet most would also agree that without anxiety creativity would die. Anxiety is just the Accountant's word for what the Mind's Eye redefines as the excitement of the chase. Fear threatens the entrepreneur's every move. When you are concentrating on walking across the razor's edge, your imagination magnifies every sensation you encounter. Frank Herbert, in *Dune*, offers this amazing "Litany Against Fear":

I must not fear. Fear is the mind-killer. Fear is the little death that brings instant obliteration. I will face my fear. I will permit it to pass over me and through me. And when it has gone past I will turn the inner eye to see its path. Where the fear has gone there will be nothing. Only I will remain.

Obviously the trick is to allow your Mind's Eye to take control of the anxiety, claiming it as your own territory, redefining it as something closer to the heart's desire without losing its effectiveness as a goad to action. Working your caduceus through vocabulary transformations, "anxiety" becomes "uncertainty" becomes "elation." Excitation is a sign of life, a good sign. Never forget that this particular rush of energy you've called anxiety is your own characteristic creation, the threshold of your dream. Honor it by renaming it in your own best image.

Talking to yourself

Cajun proverb: If you not talking to yourself, you not talking to anybody important.

Atchity: When you talk to yourself, make sure you're listening.

Others have confirmed the usefulness of talking to yourself (see, for example, Shad Helmstetter's *What To Say When You Talk to Yourself*). Talking to the Accountant and the Visionary during a moment of crisis can be enormously illuminating, though sometimes your Mind's Eye has to trick you into the conversation by jumping into the middle of one of those familiar internal debates that always seem to come out the same way.

Here's a typical example. You're sitting down at a restaurant on a business trip, alone. You aren't really that hungry, but you're telling yourself you deserve to eat something nice because you've had a hard trip. Your eyes scan the selections, one part of your brain pushing for the salad, the other pushing for the prime rib. Wait a minute, you say to yourself, how can I be thinking of the prime rib when I know it's not good for me, and would be a waste of money because I'm not even that hungry. But, the other part is saying, you deserve the prime rib. This is a great restaurant, why eat only salad? Celebrate.

Your Mind's Eye jumps into the conversation:

Mind's Eye: "Who said celebrate?"

With your Mind's Eye, you round up the usual suspects: the Accountant and the Visionary. The Accountant, because he's measuring what you deserve or don't deserve, and the price of things; the Visionary, because he's so excited by the prime rib and feels like celebrating.

If you've ever had the experience of planning in advance not to "pig out" at a meal, sticking with your plan up to the last moment, "pigging out," then having immediate remorse, what's really happening is a "Visionary override." Your Mind's Eye and Accountant know what should be done, but the Visionary, in its extreme neediness and complete lack of foresight, simply overrides all the sensibleness and takes over during the feast. Afterwards, the others click in again—too late. The Accountant grumbling that you just gained five pounds and wasted money, your Mind's Eye wondering how it lost control of the situation.

Becoming aware of who's talking is the only way to break out of this pattern. The Accountant is saying the roast beef would be a waste of money because I'm not even that hungry. But the Visionary insists, "I deserve the prime rib. This is a great restaurant, why eat only salad? Celebrate."

If awareness prevails, the Mind's Eye may finally placate Accountant and Visionary by ordering a shrimp cocktail and the salad, maybe even allowing it to be a festive Caesar salad. If the Visionary is particularly adamant, the Mind's Eye may even order the prime rib, with the stipulation that you'll eat only a few bites then ask that your plate be removed. And you feel better about yourself when you get back to your room.

It comes down to which voice will you recognize as the *best you*.

The hedonistic Visionary lives to eat; the Puritanical Accountant eats to live. Neither attitude satisfies the Type C whose Mind's Eye is determined to discover the exact balance that allows us to eat well in a celebratory manner at each meal. The Mind's Eye's discovery proceeds by jumping into the middle of these debates, and interrupting the pattern. Make the next restaurant menu you face a test of your ability to identify the various voices, and awaken your Mind's Eye to manage them to your benefit. Pick and choose. Don't be afraid to ask for half portions, or to leave half of your meal on the plate. "Eat everything on your plate" is no longer an appropriate admonition once you've left your parents' house. And money is certainly not the issue. If you can afford to eat in restaurants at all, you can afford to take liberties with the menu. In the long run it even makes economic sense for you to order several expensive but relatively healthy dishes and pick and choose what you like from them. Eat what's good for you, and what's fun, in a combination that makes long-range sense. Don't worry about being considered eccentric by your companions, by the waiter, or by the management. You are eccentric.

Energy management

Managing your energy is one of the most vital steps in the self-knowing process that leads to satisfaction in the creative life. The process begins by allowing your Mind's Eye to take an inventory of how you feel day in and day out. Most people know something about themselves in this regard: "I'm a night owl," or, "I'm a morning person." But it's also important to know which activities drain you, and which invigorate you. I schedule lectures and seminars as inter-ruptions to a long siege of writing because standing up teaching all day *invigorates* me as much as it might drain someone else. Going to meetings, on the other hand, takes energy away. I need to play tennis afterwards, or take a cold shower, or hit the treadmill to regain my energy.

Energy isn't constant, but operates on an ebb and flow principle that varies from person to person. When you're experiencing a surge of energy, it's time for reaching out—making sales calls, following up, closing, dealing with a particularly thorny challenge. When your energy is ebbing, it's time to withdraw into an activity that restores your energy—ranging from reading and writing in solitude to taking a quick nap or going for a walk.

Because your dream's success often depends upon the image you present to the public—and because you recognize the enormous energy it requires to keep this image shining when, deep down, you're exhausted from the effort—you'll learn to keep a high public profile when you're up, and to maintain a lower profile when you're down. You are, after all, selling the confidence in your voice and in your posture. Don't risk the sales call when the energy's not there.

Instincts

Before my career transit, I used to say, "I'd love to follow my instincts if I could just find the damned things." Throwing your lot into a new career restores your instincts. Because I now knew nothing about what I was going to be every day, I was forced to listen for my inner voice. I was forced to recognize and discover my own Mind's Eye. The biggest mistakes I've made in the past six years have been derived from *not* following my initial instincts, including what I call the "Life Is Too Short Response."

In order to discover your Mind's Eye, you'll have to fight the Accountant, who is fighting for the control he's used to exercising over your practical daily routine. And he'll win some if not most of the time at first. You get around him by keeping track of his responses, and comparing them to the outcome of following your Mind's Eye's instincts instead. Here's a typical example.

A woman dressed entirely in orange approaches you with her plan to introduce a new toy into the market. She has a booklet and a video clip prepared that you immediately recognize as something that should never be shown to a publisher or production company. They aren't professional, and are tattered around the edges. They are orange. She has a homemade mockup that she says was done by a company in New York. Her makeup is askew and though the day is cool she looks like she's just driven through a forest fire. After telling you her entire medical history from birth on, she explains that she wants you to take over the project, help her make the sale, help produce the book, the film, the TV series, the videos, the toys.

Despite the fact that you're not in the toy business, your Visionary sees, beneath the surface, that the idea is cute. Your Accountant adds that less cute ideas have made fortunes. Before you know it, you're talking about what you can do to help—your connections with children's book editors, your relationships with animation houses, etc. Meanwhile, your Mind's Eye is tugging at your sleeves, saying: "Life is too short."

You ignore the tugging, and six months later totally regret it. The project is a waste of time because its creator is her own worse enemy, impossible to deal with, unwilling to be pinned down to a deal, paranoid, suspicious—and probably lying about her medical record. You ease your way out of the situation, swearing to yourself that you'll listen to your instincts next time. Your Mind's Eye's gentle tugging at the sleeve was more important than the Visionary's shout or the Accountant's quiet abacus.

The next time a woman in orange arrives your Mind's Eye has a better chance of winning the argument.

If you could find the circuit box that controls self-defeating and self-sabotaging behavior like pursuing a sidetrack despite the "Life Is Too Short Response," it would be relatively easy to open it up and check the circuits.

The circuit box is your mind, and you can open it up.

Mind

Wallace Stevens: "It is never satisfied, the mind. Never."

Type C: "Maybe that's why I try to get out of my mind whenever possible."

Mood becomes attitude becomes language becomes action becomes reaction-and-results becomes a dream fulfilled. But for those educated in the traditions of Western civilization, seasoned in reason and logic, all too often dream issues first in thought. For us the progression reads: *Dream becomes thought becomes mood becomes attitude. . . .*

We all know that the mind plays tricks on us, one of the most familiar being its selective memory capacity. While we're sleeping or simply growing older our mind is busy revising scenes from the past to fit our present needs. Jung called "selective perception" that uncanny ability of the mind to see owls everywhere—on coins, coats of arms, belt buckles, and bath towels—once you've decided to write a book about owls. Psychologists call a victim's sharp recollection of the gun used to fire at them "weapon focus," as in: "I don't remember his face, but it was a .38 caliber, black-barrelled gun, with a rosewood handle." One of the worst I've come across is an actor friend who told me the story of his second divorce. "Two years into our marriage," he said, "we were having a party and I turned to introduce a guest to my wife—and couldn't remember her *name*. Jeremy, this is my wife—what'shername."

When your mind, without "your" cooperation, is able to cause traffic accidents, or to lose billfolds, wrist watches, eyeglasses, or your wife's name, obviously your Mind's Eye has not yet been discovered and put in charge. Obviously minds performing tricks like these are signaling desperately that the inner conflict must come to an end. The animals in the ring are running amok because the ringmaster is out to lunch.

Magic thinking

One of the most common tricks the untamed mind comes up with that damages the entrepreneur's career transit is "magic thinking," an extraordinary sabotage mechanism arising primarily from the Visionary, which undermines progress toward the dream. Unmastered magic thinking slows your forward momentum, and creates a very negative attitude of victimization. A typical example of magic thinking is neglecting to follow up on a solicitation, hoping that your prospect is taking a long time to answer because "it must be under serious consideration." Months go by and you finally call to follow up, only to discover that they didn't receive what you sent. Destructive magic thinking takes the adage "no news is good news" seriously. Magic thinking is finding an agent to handle your sales for you because, "I'm just not good at selling," then discovering that you're spending as much time bugging the agent as you would be bugging the potential customers—and much less productively.

The Accountant cooperates in magic thinking because the Accountant's ego hates rejection. The longer it postpones a phone call, the longer it puts off what it fears may be a negative response.

When the Mind's Eye takes over,

- We keep our sharpest, "third" eye on the ball.
- We automatically follow up every solicitation with a phone call "just to make sure you received my letter."
- We automatically construct a linkage to the next step: "When shall I bug you for your response?"
- We calendar the two weeks the prospect asked for, and, giving another day or so extra for courtesy, call back: "You asked me to call in two weeks."

Uncontrolled magic thinking has been replaced with reality-based, productive, confidence-inspiring behavior.

The Mind's Eye, as the most sophisticated of the entrepreneur's three minds, recognizes that magic thinking may indeed play a constructive role in relationship to mood and self-confidence. When you breakfast on hope every day, you must do your shopping somewhere. The more experienced you become, the more you know where to find hope at the best prices—even inventing it, if need be, by allowing some illusions to continue until a more satisfying nut falls into your bowl. Then you can discard the other, like a man who discards a shaky wooden crutch for a reinforced aluminum one. He would be foolish to discard the wooden crutch before he's got his hands on the replacement. Your Mind's Eye allows magic thinking when hope is in need of buttressing, but only to get through that low moment. Here's an example.

It's Friday afternoon. You've had a rough week of defeated expectations, and know you'll spend the weekend struggling to transform vocabulary and to revisualize your dream and goals. You haven't heard an answer from the finance group, but you did receive a message from them at lunch asking you to call them. You don't know whether that's good news or bad news. You aren't looking forward to the weekend anyway, so maybe you should call for the answer right now so you can deal with all the setbacks or negatives or whatever you call them all at once. As you reach for the phone, it rings. The news is not from the finance group, but from a customer. He wants to double his order, putting you in the black for the next two months. You hang up on a high, excited to end a tough week with good news. It's magic thinking not to make that call to the finance group, but your Mind's Eye decides magic thinking is allowable at this point because you need a positive weekend in which to regroup, remend your safety net, do contingency planning, and get your head back together. Your Mind's Eye decides that going through this process on a high, which is now possible if you don't make that phone call, is a necessary boost. Whatever you learn on Monday, you'll be able to deal with better. So it says, "Let's just assume that the news from them is good as well. We'll rebuild our strength and call them Monday."

You have a great weekend. On Monday you call to discover that they need one more piece of information, which you provide them immediately because your energy is restored.

Magic thinking is okay if your Mind's Eye approves it.

By the same token, your Mind's Eye won't let you make what could possibly be a negative phone call on your way into an important sales meeting. It preserves your performance level by keeping the blinders on. It would be self-sabotage to make that call before the meeting, and your Mind's Eye is ever-vigilant against self-sabotage.

The impostor syndrome

The question, "What makes you think you're an authority?" is bad enough when someone asks it of you. But it can be worse if you're constantly asking it of yourself. One of the mind's favorite tricks is to use logic to set logic aside. Logically, you've never produced a film before, so how can you hope to be a producer? Remember, I didn't say the Accountant was brilliant. Because, by the same logic, no one who's never produced a film before could be a producer. But producers exist, who at some point had never produced films. This "do-loop," as it's called in computer language, has been formally identified as "the imposter syndrome." The good news is that it's absolutely *normal* for you to feel like an impostor. Feeling like an impostor is a symptom that comes with exploring new territory. If you *don't* feel like an impostor, you aren't serious about your career transit.

Tricks you can play on your mind

One of the advantages of age is learning that you can outwit yourself. Your mind, though never satisfied, does becomes more or less predictable—and you can get around it when it's behaving badly.

Carl Sagan, in *The Dragons of Eden*, argues that our sharp auditory recall is a throwback to our reptilian mind when the sense of hearing was all-important for survival. When human beings evolved, we survived through our thinking. Yet we don't take our thinking as seriously as we do what we hear, see, or smell. The mundane example is the practice of repeating out loud something we want to remember. Hearing our voice say the phone number, or spell the name, imprints it more securely in memory than just thinking the name or number. That is a mind trick.

Another version of the same trick is using your voice to activate sleeping portions of the mind. When you can't remember a name, tell yourself *out loud:* "I can't remember the name." This often triggers an instant recall.

Inventory the tricks you've successfully played on your mind, and keep track of each new effort to defeat self-sabotage. One of the most important tricks I discovered years ago has been consistently effective in avoiding those little depressions we call "funks" or "slumps." I came to the conclusion that if I associated these depressions, lasting from one hour to two or three days, with something positive I might not dread them as much as I did. I made a list of things I never took the time to do, including "reading magazines" and "playing video games." I kept the list in a handy place and decided that whenever I felt depressed I'd take it out. I started looking forward to getting depressed, thinking that I'd finally get to catch up with the stacks and stacks of magazines that had accumulated—and also learn how to play the latest Nintendo games. I don't think I applied the list more than once. The little slumps simply stopped occurring. My Mind's Eye's scheme had outwitted whatever sabotage was going on between Visionary and Accountant.

Accountant: We're up Shit Creek without a paddle.

Mind's Eye: No, we're up Shit Creek *with many* paddles.

Atchity: He said it was "promising."

Friend: You can't let one adjective ruin your entire life.

Nearly everyone who writes about remotivation and career change stresses the importance of becoming aware of the words you say to yourself and to others. Whoever said, "Sticks and stones may break my bones, but words will never hurt me," was trying to divert attention from the most potent weapons. Pain for pain, we're probably hurt more by words than by any other weapon we've created. Redefining your vocabulary and choice of terms means recreating the world you live in to fit the image of your dream. Examine your own story carefully to discover those negative "iceberg words" that may be doing you in.

"I'm afraid that . . ."
"We have a real problem . . ."
"I don't see how . . ."
"It's impossible to . . ."
"Weird . . ."

You are defining and designing your life; don't forget to redesign your language. Your language defines your experience.

There's nothing right or wrong about this chart; it's personal to me, as yours will be to you. When you get good at transforming your own vocabulary, you'll even begin *seeing* words differently. One particularly dark day, I forced myself to go to a meeting despite being on the edge of despair about whether I'd ever make it in "this crazy business." The meeting was inspiring, encouraging, and lifted my spirits immeasurably. I came out to discover a note

Word Transformation Chart:

Bad Words	Neutral Words	Good Words
anxiety	uncertainty	elation
delusion	illusion	vision
rejection	pass	open door
problem, crisis	situation	opportunity
the rat race	routine	my vocation
mercurial	flexible	spontaneous
I'm quitting	I'm stalled	I'm regrouping
impossible	difficult	interesting
fear	concern	challenge
failure	stall	learning curve
impediment	consideration	challenge
defeat	setback	turning point
worry	problem	challenge
blame	responsibility	credit
confused	uncertain	reassessing
weird	weird	weird

on the windshield of my car. The note, in writing as jagged as it was sincere, said: "YOU ARE ON A ONE WAY STREET!" I'd been too upset to read my newspaper horoscope that morning, and had missed my fortune cookie for breakfast, so I immediately took this as a further sign that I was heading in the right direction—that my dream was within reach. When I got into the car and turned on the ignition, I noticed that I was facing traffic heading for me in both lanes. "I get it," I finally said. The note meant I'm on a one way street. I carefully backed into a driveway, to turn back with the traffic, wondering whether my unconscious was issuing warnings again.

The never-satisfied mind

I was taught to be a perfectionist, but in a practical way. One hundred percent is the goal, but we aim for it with the foreknowledge that we're human and will never reach 100%, or if we do, we will maintain it only temporarily. Yet 100% is a better goal than 88%, because if 88% is your goal you'll *never* hit 90%. So 100% is a better goal as long as you understand that goals are almost by definition unreachable because the enterprising goal-seeker will have set a second goal by the time he accomplishes the first. If your goal is to finance a $30 million real estate development, by the time you've closed your deal for $28.6 million you'll be so busy planning your $75 million dollar deal you won't be upset that you "fell short" by $1.4 million.

But the 100% standard is used by the Accountant as a superb sabotage mechanism. The Accountant uses the argument of "quality vs quantity": "Yes, I know you could rush to production with this new Visionary invention. But a million things can go wrong with it down the road and it's better to troubleshoot them all before you make yourself an enormous laughingstock with an equally enormous liability. Let's do a quality job." So the Accountant proceeds to supervise an endless troubleshooting expedition, that tunes, fine-tunes, and re-tunes the invention to the point that it's no longer recognizable; or until someone else goes public with the same invention. "But I want it to be 100% perfect," it argues when the Mind's Eye scolds it. "We'll settle for 98%," replies the Mind's Eye, realizing that such a compromise is required if we're going to reap the benefits of the Visionary's great idea.

Without losing the spirit of the quest for excellence, the perfectionist, also known as "the judge" or "the critic", must be tamed if you are to accomplish your goals, objectives, and dreams. How do you know when to stop fine-tuning? You don't. Work can go on indefinitely. Yet set a deadline, beyond which you will cease fine-tuning and begin mass production.

Bridling the imagination

Albert Einstein: Imagination is more important than knowledge.

Pablo Picasso: Everything you can imagine is real.

Atchity: Imagination is the entrepreneur's best friend—and worst enemy.

The Type C mind is constantly troubled by imagination, that Visionary breeding ground. As the Accountant uses perfection to sabotage progress, the Visionary never ceases to provide images to the Mind's Eye's screen. The damned thing just won't stop, like the little old lady in the shoe.

At one point I was determined to learn to take naps, just to get away from it all, and so that I could stay up later and get up earlier without losing what was then left of my mind. I'd never been able to nap on airplanes, in cars, or even in the comfort of my own bed. I remembered that my mother was a champion napper, able to nap even in the midst of a lagging conversation. Her naps ranged in duration from several seconds to an hour, and she always awakened refreshed. So I called her for advice.

"Mom, I'm ready to get serious about napping. What's your secret?"

"I just imagine I'm a stick of butter, slowing melting on the stove. And then I melt into sleep."

"Great," I said. "I'll try it."

She called a few days later to ask how it had gone. "It was a complete disaster," I said. "First I imagined the butter on the butter dish. Then it started melting. Then it started spilling over the sides of the dish onto the griddle, then down into the hole into the oven. Then the oven was filled with black smoke, and the kitchen filled with smoke, until I could smell the smoke—"

She interrupted me. "You know you've always had an overactive imagination," she said. "You're too intense."

How do you quiet the imagination? By telling it to shut up. I'm serious. Your Mind's Eye has the authority and power to say, "Go away," to that agitated and unruly Visionary who won't stop its yammering. That's what discipline is all about. You say to yourself (that is, your Mind's Eye says to your Visionary): "That's enough out of you for today. Your ideas are great, but we're about to go off-line and we'll check with you tomorrow." Or you find something else, like reading, to do with your mind until the yammering diminishes. It's a question of who's to be the master. The very same mind that's been causing you all the trouble can be a wonderful co-worker once it's ring-mastered by your Mind's Eye.

Eliminate self-doubt

Atchity: How do you manage not to take your situation seriously?

Friend: I just refuse to internalize every fucking problem I've created for myself.

One of the Mind's Eye's first tasks is the elimination of the constant self-questioning that institutionalizes itself as self-doubt. The functional entrepreneur runs a daily search-and-destroy mission to eliminate the negative influences that lead you to question what you're doing. Living in dread of the end of the world is narcissistic self-involvement instead of the kind of positive self-investment it takes to make dreams come true. People with much less going for them than you have succeeded in living peacefully within their dreams, fulfilling their potential. Lack of self-confidence is everyone's enemy—from the most consistent failures to the most successful winners. But acting from lack of self-confidence is unnecessary, and an impediment to your forward progress.

Blame is also a waste of time. There's nothing you can

do about the mistakes you've made in the past, and spending valuable mental time blaming yourself for them is just as futile as spending time blaming others. Whatever happened, just move forward. One of my clients had an enormous breakthrough when he decided that his entire past life was a swamp on which he, an alien en route to a bright new planet, had just landed temporarily. He determined to regard the swamp simply as a "given" he had to operate on while collecting what he needed to complete his voyage to the bright new planet. Any time spent probing into the swamp, he decided, was wasted. He's been able to steal vast amounts of time simply by refusing to look backwards.

In the same family of time-devourers, indecisiveness ranks high. It's not a vice for most Type Cs, but it creeps into the lives of some to throw them into a tailspin that swallows up weeks and months. There are two kinds of good decisions: good decisions, and bad decisions. A bad decision is almost as good as a good one because, once made, we quickly learn that it is bad and are able to begin the self-correcting process. The truly bad decision is the one that's postponed; because no self-correction, and consequently no forward movement, occurs. Learn to make the best decision you can with the facts at hand, review it for a predetermined amount of time, then put it into action, trusting yourself to correct errors in judgment as soon as you recognize them.

How often do I re-evaluate?

Harry Truman: If you can't stand the heat, get out of the kitchen.

Atchity: Get out of the kitchen just long enough to regain your appetite.

The person in career transit re-evaluates every day. But re-evaluation is not the same as indecisiveness. Let's call it instead "review and adjustment" of the game plan for the sake of confirming its validity and improving its focus based on new data. The important thing to remember is that you reevaluate your objectives before your goals, and your goals before your dream. If you find yourself constantly re-evaluating your dream, you haven't yet made the commitment. Dreams are costly, and should not be pursued without the certainty that they are desired with your whole being.

One of the positive side-effects of this daily re-evaluation is that it automatically turns the anxiety you're feeling into that "productive elation" you now recognize as the natural result of your commitment to your goal. Getting out of the kitchen is a vacation from the center of the storm, where it's sometimes impossible for you to maintain your perspective. In the midst of the woods, you're so blinded by the thick trees of detail you've forgotten which way is forward and which is backwards. Vacations allow you to escape being done in by the details that preoccupy you in the kitchen's heat. You get out long enough to re-evaluate, refocus, regroup your energies so that you can come right back into the heat refreshed and hungry for your dream to continue.

Concentration

The label on your career transit says, "Concentrate." As in tennis, the only way to win comes from keeping your eye on the ball.

At another turning point, I called my French-Louisianan uncle Wilbur, who had always been my counselor in the family, to explain that I hadn't spoken with him "for ages" because I'd been "under the gun." He asked me enough specific questions to assess that my state of mind was quite fragile, too fragile to risk on conversations that might prove negative. We managed to visit through jokes and ended the phone call quickly. But a few days later, I received a wonderful card from him.

I know you have been going through some trying times. Hopefully things will come all together soon. Please don't ever give up, as long as there is one small ray of hope. Like a good captain, stay on your ship and keep the sails up and ready. The breeze you need to touch your sails may be just a calm moment away, and may soon come to blow all your dreams into reality.

You are in the troubled straits of career transit, straits you've never navigated before. Bad enough that the cliffs are jagged, and erratically jutting into the narrow waterway. Bad enough that there are lethal rocks hidden beneath the surface. Suddenly you find yourself, hands already blue-knuckled on the wheel, in a torrential downpour. Visibility is reduced to zero. You can't even see the surface of the water, much less the cliffs, much less the surface distortions caused by the submerged rocks. Then the compass is shattered by lightning. What do you do? Well, as tempting as it may be, jumping ship is probably a terrible idea. You've gone so far now it's easier to proceed than to abandon or turn back. The only logical thing to do is to maintain composure in the present, Keep your hands firmly on the wheel, following your instincts about the movements of the ship and the storm—and simply do the best you can. That's what being the captain of your own dream is all about.

Dreamwork

Joseph Campbell: Myth is public dream; dream is private myth.

Atchity: I'm taking my dream public.

The entrepreneur engaged in a heroic quest into the unknown country of career transit is living his private myth every day. It stands to reason that he should know it directly by getting in touch with his dreams. How could your own unconscious *not* be useful to you? The brain is an image factory that never stops processing images: receiving them from out there, storing them, recombining them, remembering them sometimes, forgetting them often, creating them, sending them back out again in a perpetual motion kaleidoscope.

Rather than puzzling over their meaning and allowing an unresolved feeling to nag you and force you to ignore your dreams, you can consult with your dreams for corroboration of your mission in life as well as the answer specific questions you have. This practice was known to the Greeks and Romans as "dream incubation." They built temples where people would go to spend the night specifically for the purpose of consulting the gods of sleep and dream.

It was about two years into my career change when I spent the weekend at Gayle Delaney's and incubated the dream of the serpents. The incubation question was, "Am I doing the right thing?" Though I had just finished producing 16 films, my financial situation seemed not better but worse. The problems were bigger, the solutions seemed as out of reach as they had *before* the deal was finally made.

The first night's dream was something like this: *I'm on a ledge high up on a cliff wall, in pain, realizing I'm afraid of heights* (for some reason, this recurring dream always reveals my fear of *getting down*, never of *going up*). *I look up the cliff and see that the wall between me and the top is all broken glass. I can't go up. I look down and see that the cliff below is also broken glass. No wonder I'm in pain. What to do? Going down would be as painful as going up. Then I look at the ledge on which my bleeding feet are standing, and realize it's covered with broken glass as well.* Was this a helpful dream? It was so brief a vision, it seemed insignificant.

The next morning, at breakfast, Gayle wanted to hear what I dreamed. And I told her. She helped me realize that the dream was, in fact, very significant. The only thing hopeful and positive and firm in the dream was my choice. I had *chosen* a painful climb. Going down made no sense because it offered only more pain with no reward. Standing still made no sense for the same reason. Climbing to the top, through whatever pain lay in wait, was the only alternative. As I do for my clients, Gayle played the role of the Mind's Eye for me, sorting out the meaning of this dream that seemed to encapsulate my Accountant's anxieties.

The next night I dreamed that *I was on an immense football field, dwarfed by the giant players marching back and forth against me. I had no idea what I was doing on the field because I wasn't a football player. I was wearing the uniform of a soccer player, not protected, as the giants were, by padding. Yet I managed to dodge in and out of them, kicking the ball along as I went.* Gayle led me to interpret this dream by asking me first how I felt when I woke up. I told her I felt great. I *was* on a strange playing field in this new film business I'd entered into. Although I wasn't equipped like the giants on the field for a game familiar to them, I was able to survive and make my way through the game because I had skills that were useful in this regard. I was feeling like an impostor, in other words, precisely because in a very real sense I *was* an impostor—going where I'd never gone before, as *Star Trek* puts it. The best thing about the dream was its reminder that I was on a playing field, playing a game. I had *chosen* my career change. No one was forcing me to have the problems I was having. If I could give myself perspective, by accepting my Mind's Eye's definition of what I was doing as a *game*, the pain might become more bearable. It was simply a matter of understanding the rules, knowing the objectives of the game, and using what skills I'd developed in my previous career to play as well as possible at any given moment.

Sometimes I employ a local hotel as my incubation temple. I used to make a practice of spending New Year's Eve alone at a new hotel in Los Angeles each year, taking only my journals with me to end the old year with reflection and to begin the New Year with resolve. And, before going to sleep, I would ask my dreams for a vision of how I was doing.

Meditation

John Lennon: Life is what happens to you while you're busy making other plans.

Zen: Do not look for the way. You are already there.

Atchity: You have to come home often to appreciate the journey.

Sooner or later, people committed to changing themselves as a way of life turn to meditation, of one sort or the other, as an aid to "being there," being centered and present to the full intensity of your chosen life. No matter how complicated the various gurus make it seem, its bottomline value is that it stills the mind. More specifically, meditative breathing quiets the Accountant's constant shuttling of worry beads back and forth on his abacus, and the Visionary's screams of delighted discovery. The inner voices that won't stop jabbering do stop during successful meditation, allowing your Mind's Eye to rise from the battlefield and find the tranquillity of perspective. David Richo's *How To Be an Adult* offers a clear and simple guide to meditation that will suit the western mind. A 15-minute meditation session in the middle of the typically crazy entrepreneurial day can do wonders for setting you back on course.

The Type C's astronomical event horizon

Kenneth Burke: Mankind is huddled together, nervously loquacious, at the edge of an abyss.

Atchity: And what if the black hole is inside me?

Director Mort Ransen and I were talking about the weird life of the entertainment world one evening. One of its frustrations, he grumbled, is that its "event horizon" is "astronomical." I asked him to explain. He was referring to the moment at which matter either escapes from or disappears into a black hole, the black hole being failure, the escape being success. But so few tangible successes occur in the entrepreneur's life: an acquisition deal actually closing, a finance deal actually closing, a star actually committing to a date when the money is actually available. A film finally being shot. A film finally being released. The rest is chatter and disappearances. The rest is straining your eyes at the telescope, trying to convince yourself that you will see a new constellation forming if you concentrate hard enough and long enough.

If your career transit has similar characteristics, don't forget that the event horizon began as *your* dream; the astronomical chart is your chart, your Vision of what you could be. You've seen a possible future and begin behaving as though that future were real. Before long, people begin catching the spirit and moving with you toward that future.

From time to time, the future looms on the horizon— sometimes as shadow, sometimes with almost tangible substance. When you perceive it as shadow, you feel the depths of despair; when you feel its presence clearly, an unimagined elation washes over you. It may help to keep in mind the business principle: *No news means no news.* Don't make things worse by *imagining* what's not there.

One of the systems I've invented to provide some sort of radar coverage of the event horizon is recording in my day runner *green lights* and *red lights*, positive events in green ink and negative events in red. On a typical day, five green lights occur and generally no more than one red light. A green light is defined as a "good sign" that a particular objective is making progress. A red light is an event that makes an objective no longer possible.

Green lights for me include:

• Distributor agrees to create budget for *Dead South*
• Signed new client

- NBC picks up *Unwanted Attentions*
- Library agrees to do weekend workshops
- Finished script!

These are my *red lights:*

- Audit notice from IRS
- Distributor refuses to give quarterly accounting
- Jerry drops out of workshop

Recording these lights in tandem with transforming your vocabulary becomes increasingly encouraging. You see that the greens are winning partly because you're transforming setbacks into challenges, delays into opportunities. The audit is an opportunity to fight one of the darkest dragons, and to find out if you're up to it. The distributor's refusal is a challenge that you'll meet more than once along the way. Here's the chance to deal with it. Jerry dropping out means he's in some kind of trouble. Let's see what we can do to help him privately.

Take credit for the fact that the entire process wouldn't be occurring if it weren't for your daring. If it weren't for your dream, and your determination to pursue it. The dream will never come true if you stop believing in it. You are its sole and sufficient creator, and destroyer. If you continue, you *can* deal with whatever occurs on the event horizon.

How do you measure success?

Dealing with this frustrating event horizon really forces you to reevaluate your definition of success. Wouldn't it be a shame if you created your dreamworld out of elements unique to you, then failed to enjoy it because you were *measuring* it by someone else's standards? If you are in a difficult new career where financial success comes rarely and only with extraordinary good luck added to outstanding performance, don't make the mistake of measuring your success by where you now stand financially. If this is a creative career, measure your success by your creative accomplishments; and, yes, survival may be the chief among them. You may not have made money on your first film, but it has your name on it. It's a "credit"—you're in the ballpark. Only three customers arrived on your antique store's opening day, but the doors are open, and you're *in business.* More than anything else, measure your success by the satisfaction that you feel yourself and the recognition accorded you by others, sometimes begrudgingly, that you are "doing your thing" and "following your bliss."

I know of no better definition than that of Thomas Carlyle, who called success "continual progress toward a worthy goal."

Ups and downs

Laurence Sterne: There must be *ups* and *downs*, or how the duce should we get into vallies where Nature spreads so many tables of entertainment.

Atchity: I don't want to lose my humility.

Best friend: Yeah, you do. You can't wait.

Maybe I like roller coasters because my life is a roller coaster. "If one advances confidently in the direction of his dreams,"

Henry David Thoreau said, in *Walden*, "he will meet with a success unexpected in common hours." The elations are indeed outstanding. But unless you redefine success as Carlyle defines it, you'll find the downslides terrifying and generally all-round unbearable. You must see them as part of the very fiber of your success.

Once self-mastery gets him up and running, the entrepreneur meets with moments of success each and every day—finding a new corner to cut, handling a difficult phone call, deferring an impossible payment, finding a way to reduce costs. Let's make sure that we learn to recognize these moments, to savor them, to learn from them. Remember that success is in *process*, not in product or result.

Mastering the downgrades is obviously an important key to making your Type C behavior your greatest success. After all, the great thing about being "down" is that you've nowhere to go but up. You know you will go up. Part of your mind—your Mind's Eye—knows it. So, if necessary, get into being down, remembering the line from *King Lear*: "The worst is never so long as we can say, this is the worst." When all else fails, embrace depression and bottom out with a preconstructed safety net. As the phoenix would say, "Once more, dear friends, into the ashes!"

Why are things so difficult? Because you've chosen a difficult path in order to challenge yourself, and to expand your potential. You are building character during these downcycles, the character that will serve you well when you are on your way up again, and when you have reached the plateau you're dreaming of. Proof of this is what often happens to those who "get lucky" and experience precocious success. They don't know what to do with it, blow it all, and find themselves without the character resilience to make a comeback. So count yourself lucky when things go sour from time to time. It's your dream making sure you're worthy of it.

The downcycles are often simply reminders that you can't control everything. You can only move the ball when it's in your court, and have little control over others. Letting go of the pretense that you're in control is a huge step forward. When something unplanned occurs, take it as a sign that there are powers greater than you in charge and that it's all right to allow them to move you instead of your constantly attempting to move them. Because you've relied so much on planning, you will begin to *enjoy* the unplanned with particular relish.

8
Dealing with People:
Family, Spouses, Best Friends, Ex-friends, Associates, Winners, Losers, Saviors, Nay-sayers, White Knights, Black Knights, Clay Gods, and the Little Red Hen

Shakespeare: The friends thou hast, and their affection tried,/Grapple them to thy soul with hoops of steel.

Atchity: The friends you had, their affection getting strained, replace those hoops with elastic banks. Be only with people with whom you can be yourself.

Nothing is more important to the career transit entrepreneur than maintaining a positive support group. Without it, chances are you'll find yourself burning out and, unlike the phoenix, having no strength to rise from the ashes. Career transit success involves redefining all the people in your life by reference to your dream. They fall into three categories: good guys, bad guys, and guys who'd better declare themselves before you place them in the bad guy category. A good guy, by Visionary definition, is a family member, spouse, or friend who tells you to "Go for it!" and who reminds you to "believe in yourself," reassuring you that you have the strength to overcome the problems you've freely chosen. Bad guys are those who are worried about the decision you're making, and who never let go of their worried warnings even when you are years into the transition. Often the bad guy *liked* what you were before you made the switch. You were a good professor, why are you sabotaging yourself by changing?

Unfortunately the bad guy can be your father or mother, your child, your spouse, or your longtime friend. Weeks before I announced my resignation from Occidental College, I held a cocktail party at my home for nearly a hundred people. It was a kind of unofficial *sayonara* party to mark my transition. At the height of the party, an older professor who had been a close friend through the years came up to me and said, "Well, how does it feel to be an immoral businessman?"

"Exactly how it felt to be an immoral professor," I should have replied, but didn't.

The question floored me because it came from someone I very badly wanted to keep in my "good guy" set.

I opened a UCLA seminar on career change for actors and actresses once by asking, "What is the question you hate to hear most at cocktail parties, and how do you answer it?"

The first actress said, "The question I hate most it, 'When are you going to move back to Detroit and take a job with the post office?'"

"How do you answer it?" I asked.

"I usually burst into tears and leave the party."

I told her I understood, then moved on to the second actress. She said the question she hated most was, "What have you been in big lately that I've seen?" And she answered: "The Pacific Ocean."

The difference between these two career transit individuals is that one had figured out how to defend herself against the bad guys, and the other had not. Sticks and stones are not your enemy, but casual words that come from friendly people are often the toughest obstacles of career transit.

One day, driving through the San Joaquin Valley back to Los Angeles, I had time to think about something very sad and resolve my future actions regarding it. Two particular friends had been calling recently, and I did not want to call them back. In one case it always meant "making nice" on the phone then my sidestepping the idea of setting a specific date for getting together. In the second case, even the phone call wasn't so nice. The second friend always found a way of making digs, and I always reacted badly to them, and the call always ended badly. The first had a pattern of inviting me to dinner in his faraway neighborhood (because he couldn't drive), which I always paid for (because it had long ago been established between us that I was better off than he), at a restaurant of his choice (because he had a list of dietary restrictions), while I listened to his latest tales of woe. I found myself thrilled when he'd reached only my answering machine, and equally thrilled when I reached his. In the interests of friendship, I continued seeing him, despite the fact that each time I did I felt scared. Scared by the "but for the grace of God go I" syndrome. In my own darkest imagination, I had seen myself as "down and out" as this friend; and it didn't create a positive reality for me to witness exactly how down and out that was.

I always drove home asking myself what distinguished the two of us, I a cock-eyed dreamer determined to create a better future, and he someone hoping I would do that right away so I could help him. I finally realized that both "friendly associates" were what Judith Viorst calls "necessary losses," and I needed to govern myself accordingly. In the next few years, I allowed one to drift away without returning his calls, and confronted the other with the truth that we had simply gone different ways with our lives. Eventually we found more comfortable ways of communicating, mostly by postcard.

Temporary friends vs life friends

Perhaps nothing is more distressing in career change than the inevitable necessity of leaving behind people you regarded, in your previous career, as "life friends." One of the problems is that, in the rush of initial enthusiasm, we don't bother to define the concept of friends very carefully. Life friends are the ones who are left when nothing else is working out, who stick with you when you're at your lowest, and when you're at your worst. I'm happy to say that I'm fortunate to have a few friends who have become even closer during the long career change I've undertaken. They are life friends.

The friends who've fallen behind weren't *false* friends; they were temporary friends, mistaken at the time for life friends and now seen in retrospect for what they were. There's nothing wrong with leaving temporary friends behind. Should you run into them, your greetings will be warm, your memories mutually endearing, your affection apparently intact. But the feeling of dissatisfaction and self-questioning you experience as you walk away from such a chance encounter needs attention. It's normal. It happens to all of us, as those who make it a habit of attending high school or college reunions can attest. The dissatisfaction doesn't stem from the present situation; it stems from your past being out of synch with your future.

Petrarch: I have learned that complaints are useless, that nothing avails but patience, in the things we cannot change.

Atchity: Okay, but what about a little whining?

Motivational experts tell you, "Don't complain!" I would add, "Just find someone to whine to when you need to." The life friend is that someone. When you whine, he says, "That's okay. I know it's tough. But you're doing great. You've chosen these problems, and you're getting through them." The person who responds to your whining with warnings and, "I told you so's," or, "That's just what I was worried would happen," is *not* being a friend to the entrepreneur dedicated to pursuing his dream.

Negative people and positive people

The pressures of career change are so great that you can't afford to spend your time or energy with negative people, which is what some of the temporary friends have become in your new life. If a friendly associate from the past falls into that category, sooner or later one of two things will happen: you'll either leave him behind once and for all; or you'll be dragged back into the past. You need every bit of positivity you can muster to continue marching forward into your dreamworld. Marsha Sinetar (*Do What You Love, The Money Will Follow*) admonishes:

To the extent that we accept our own greatness, the mission and charter for our own life, we want to work against anything— either external (in society or through the actions and efforts of others) or internal (our own "enemies within")—that would hold us back.

Those who aid and abet your dream are the positive people, whether they do it through psychological support or financial investment. Those who counter your dream, questioning it, blocking it, resenting it, demanding explanations for it, are enemies of the dream. Recognizing them as such allows you to "do the right thing," finding a humane way of parting with them when you can't transform them into being a positive force for you.

Every transaction between people is a contract of some sort, and a contract must be a two-way street or it doesn't last very long. You give a dollar to a homeless woman on the corner as you go into the video store. She smiles and thanks you. You feel better about yourself. The contract is minimal, but it's clear nonetheless. The next day, she's there again. You're torn. Another dollar for another smile? Maybe. But as days go by if the smile is all you're getting you feel odd about the outgoing dollars. You'd rather contribute to a charity where something definite is done to improve the future prospects of the recipients. The woman on the corner isn't making discernible progress from your dollar. The people who loiter around your bandwagon can be divided into those who help it roll and those who slow it down so they can get on. The ones you define as "positive" are the former, as "negative," the latter.

"Missionary work" is something we all do *pro bono*, nurturing and supporting those less fortunate than ourselves. But when missionary work becomes so all-consuming that it interferes with your dream, you're kidding yourself about its altruistic nature. You're avoiding your own potential, sabotaging the visionary within. Choose your missions carefully. Select activities that allow you to give back to the world without expecting immediate return, and concentrate your charitable instincts on them instead of diffusing them throughout your life.

Just like the advice for dating, "It doesn't get any better!" the advice for dealing with people in business is, Follow your initial instincts. If you don't like or trust or feel good about someone, and have confirmed this feeling with a second opinion, don't do business with them. Assume that there are enough good, positive people in the world who'll recognize the value of your dream; and realize that making deals with the wrong ones just uses up time. If you're free of the bad guys, the good guys have a chance to meet you. If you're tied up with the bad guys, the good guys deal with others.

A client once realized that she'd never be able to work on her novel during November and December, because the holidays always brought her together with her mother, who constantly pointed out that she could barely *spell* much less write. Knowing she had a deadline to meet, I asked her, "What are you going to do about it?" Rather than allowing her to answer, I urged her to think about it and tell me at our next meeting. When she came in the next week, she said, "I can't believe I did it."

"What did you do?"

"I told my mother I wasn't coming for the holidays."

"Did you tell her why?"

"No, she didn't ask."

She remained true to herself, avoided her mother, and finished her novel by January. Of course she experienced the "ghost of guilt." But I pointed out to her that experiencing that was preferable to experiencing the disgust she normally felt when she put herself in her mother's negative sphere of influence.

When you take such self-protective actions to nurture your dreams, giving them preference over your past problems, amazing things occur. Her mother started getting interested in her book, and managed to ask about it in a positive way. When she realized my client's dedication was strong enough to confront even her enormous influence, the mother came around to her daughter's side. The mother had figured out the strength of her daughter's dream, and decided she didn't want to be relegated to the negative column. She wanted to join the bandwagon.

After a seminar at Villanova, I encountered one of my Yale professors who I hadn't seen for 20 years. Over slices of his exquisite homemade wheatberry bread he told me he was concerned for his daughter, a struggling actress in New York. He had been supporting her, but was beginning to think that he should urge her to "do something practical," since she was experiencing a very long dry spell. I advised him to withhold that advice, and instead to ask her if she still believed in her career. If she said "Yes," he should express his undying support for her. "Not financial support," I added. "That's not required of you." I explained to him that for a Type C unqualified emotional support is the lifeblood of daily renewal. When self-confidence flags, the support of loved ones provides a transfusion that gets you through your mood. If your daughter decides she's ready to give it up, you can support her in a "more practical" decision. But in the meantime don't worry about her examining the alternatives. The entrepreneur's inboard Mind's Eye examines the alternatives proposed by his Accountant so thoroughly and so constantly that he doesn't need to hear the recitation of practicalities from someone whose support for the dream is vital.

Once, in a particularly painful financial stage of my career transit, my mother, who had inspired me originally, and whose emotional, psychological, and financial support had filled in so many gaps over the years, fell into the pattern of becoming the "bad guy." I was in Kansas City to visit a client who wanted to make the transition from the clothing industry (he was a "garment diverter," who had made a small fortune intercepting brand label shipments intended for one retailer and reselling them for a higher price to another). My mother wanted to know how come this man had so much money. When I explained to her what he did to earn it, she said, "You know, you'd be good at doing that." Buzz. . . . Wrong answer, Mom. I had to correct her, and set her back on course. "What I need from you, Mom, is your support and encouragement. I am not going to starve to death. I would, in fact, prefer to starve to death than to do something other than my dream." Don't expect your positive support group to be perfect. They're human, like you, and allowed to falter once in awhile. Supporting you can be as exhausting for them as continuing the quest is for you.

Sometimes we need to give the people around us a *chance* to adjust to our dream. Friends are coming for the weekend unexpectedly. You're torn between putting in three hours on Saturday morning on your dream, and "doing the right thing" for your friends. You do the right thing, entertaining them by dragging them to Six Flags. They notice you're grumpy. You may or may not confess why, but you certainly know why: you'd rather be doing what you dreamed of doing. The friends pick up on your mood, its reasons, and feel guilty; the day deteriorates. Or, your friends announce they're coming. You tell them you're always delighted to see them, and look forward to spending some time with them. "Meanwhile, I hope you guys can entertain yourselves Saturday morning. I've got some drawings to go over with my architect, and we're under a deadline."

"Are you sure we're not imposing?" they ask.

"Not at all, if you don't mind my being out of pocket a few hours."

When they hear that you mean it, they say, "Hey, we're old enough to take care of ourselves. In fact, we'd love to sit around the pool while you're gone. Don't worry about us. We'll get lunch ready if you'd like. . . . We can't wait to hear about your project when you get a chance to tell us." You feel good about their coming, and good about yourself. You've given them the opportunity to adjust to your dreamworld, to involve themselves in it by understanding. They feel good because you're accepting them into your new life without making them the bad guys.

You can also make use of the triadic mind to help transform the less-than-positive people around you into ones who will support your dream. Tell them about the Accountant, the Visionary, and the Mind's Eye. Ask them which part of them is responding to you the way they are. Often it's their own desire to lead a Type C life that underlies their negativity, and bringing them awareness is all that's needed to alter their behavior toward you. "Your Accountant is telling me that, isn't it?" you say. "I'll bet your Visionary would agree with me, if you'd just let me explain what I'm doing to your Mind's Eye." Since everyone experiences the three voices to one extent or another, this will almost always get their attention.

Nay-sayers and grumbling soldiers

In avoiding those who don't recognize and affirm your ability to reach your dream, don't confuse "grumbling soldiers" with "nay-sayers." Some people always complain. It's just their nature. You don't need their good mood, you need their assistance. Don't expect them to change their nature just because you're suddenly involved. But watch what people do instead of what people say. One of my best Yale professors was a grumbling soldier, who nonetheless managed, in his thoroughness and precision, to be totally inspiring in a very difficult subject.

The nay-sayers, on the other hand, may be cheerful in demeanor but their attitude "sucks." You go to them for advice, and they say: "You're so bright, I don't understand why you've gotten yourself into this new career. Why don't you do something easier?" You've encountered them before: they are the bad guys.

The limited marriage

I don't mean to suggest that you can't deal with the "bad guys" at all. You take what you can get from them without marrying them, and discard the rest. You tell them, "I didn't come to you for career counseling, I came to ask you a specific question." You remain in control of the relationship.

My brother Fred always said that even if someone is eight-ninths bad, he could find one-ninth that's useful in advancing business. But that approach means retaining your perspective, and refraining from prematurely "jumping into bed" with someone you have less than a perfect response to.

I call this the "limited marriage," and find it infinitely preferable to "full marriages" in business. Never throw your entire business lot in with one party. That is a sure way of sabotaging yourself, and abdicating your role as hero of your own story. You have more control over your career transit if you have many alliances on individual projects and contracts and deals than if you have one "grand alliance." You are married to your dream. You are "related" to others whose dreams are compatible with yours, and who therefore can assist you in advancing your dream more rapidly, by their cooperating in a given objective of your operating plan, than you can advance it alone.

A corollary of the limited marriage principle is this: Seek the *right kind* of help from the *right people* on the *right terms*. It takes a while to figure out how to identify each of these categories. But once you do, you'll move forward with greater assurance and with greater integrity to your dream. If your instincts are telling you that the other person is a complete skunk, forget even a limited marriage. Follow the Cajun advice: "A skunk's territory ain't worth negotiating."

When to avoid the winners

I'd like to agree with the motivational experts who say, "Never—not even when you're feeling down and out and know that being with them at the New Year's football games will make you feel worse." The theory being that, simply by faking the self-confidence to be with them, you're actually being a winner. They will recognize you're down but they won't count you out.

Nonsense. This approach doesn't work when you're miserable. And you can expect to be miserable from time to time along the way, despite everything you can do to control your mood and change your vocabulary. If you think that spending New Year's Day with the "winners" will set you back, interfering with your motivation, then by all means follow your instinct. Being with the winners and feeling like you're losing isn't good for anyone at the party. It takes enormous self-confidence to enjoy someone else's success when you're being beaten over the head by obstacles so that all you can see are the wrong kinds of stars. If you're serious about making a career transit based on your dream, no one can expect you to *be* self-confident all the way through. The important thing is simply to keep moving forward, even if that means taking occasional side trips to regain your sanity—and hiding out from the winners long enough to get your spirits back up.

Of course, what I've said earlier about going to meetings when you're feeling down applies here as well. When you do force yourself to hang out with those who've already attained their dream, even on a day when you see yours slipping away over the horizon, fate has a way of encouraging you. Something will almost surely happen at the party, a contact you might never have otherwise made, a piece of information of incalculable value, a snatch of conversation that gives you the perspective you thought you needed to go to the mountaintop to find. Try it, you'll see.

Network only with the right people

"Networking," that buzz word of motivational seminars, may indeed be an essential part of career change, although it should be done with intelligence and caution, and not for the wrong reasons. Too many networking meetings are used by those who attend them purely for socializing. Instead of helping the quest, they distract you from accomplishing your objectives.

Nor will networking with the wrong people advance your quest. If you find yourself the object of all attention at such a meeting, you're probably at the wrong meeting. I spoke one evening at a women's support group in New Orleans where the atmosphere was thick with intense networking. After my talk, one of the women asked me, "How much networking did you do in your career change?" I was surprised to hear my own answer: "Not much." I hadn't gone to seminars (except the ones I gave), hadn't attended conferences, belonged to no support groups— although after a visit with Barbara Sher (*Wishcraft*) I longed to have a support group that would really "understand" what I was doing and could truly support me. But each time I'd been moved to join one, I pulled back. Networking with the wrong people is worst than not networking at all. I'd much rather read a book.

Although I've had the pleasure of speaking at many successful, positive groups, too many support groups support losing. That's why the winners who emerge stop attending. Once, in Houston, I spoke at a Saturday morning group. After my talk, the leader of the group asked me what I'd thought of the session. "If you want my honest opinion,"

I said, "I thought your group was in danger of becoming very depressing." He sounded surprised until I pointed out all the self-demeaning humor characterizing the group's individual reports of their monthly progress. "I see what you mean," he said. "How can we fix that?" I suggested that the group adopt a rule that every report must be a *progress* report, in which the individual first details the steps forward he's taken in the last month, and only after doing so is allowed to lightheartedly explain what he had to overcome to make that step.

The networking meeting that's useful is usually one in which you can meet people who are further along the road you're taking than you are.

My networking, instead, was largely "one on one." It came from reading books and corresponding with authors who interested me, which has led to some wonderful letters and phone calls that have been tremendously supportive; finding directories appropriate to my business and searching them for signs of any contact I could use; writing letters; and finding introductions through friends. I've been lucky enough to have more than one mentor along the way. I heartily recommend that you find someone either to model yourself upon in your new enterprise, or to advise you as you reach for your goals, or both.

Here are some general tips about networking.

- *Do it in your own way.* If you're not a social person but know the party you're invited to will offer outstanding contacts, go to the party but be content with making only a single contact without worrying about "working the room." I've never failed to make an interesting contact at a party, but I've never tried to make more than one—though sometimes you make several. I feel more comfortable this way.

- *Create a method for keeping track of your contacts, and keeping them up to date by contributing something to their lives.* I send out "Door to Door," a collection of favorite trivia and conversation and cartoons I collect through the year. When people don't receive it, they call me to find out why. I keep a computerized mailing list, and let my contacts know about a forthcoming film, book reading, or lecture.

- *Go to the top.* If you see something that interests you, find out who's in charge and write or call them. This isn't always appropriate (sometimes you can receive vital insights from someone who's not at the top), but it's always a good idea to consider the "chief" as a first approach.

- *Identify the human interests of your "network."* They are people, not "opportunities." Eat with them, laugh with them, share their personal interests.

- *Realize that a small, vital network is more effective than a large, loosely organized group that you can't possibly keep up with.* For one thing, you *can't* get to know a thousand people personally. You *can* get to know 20 or 30.

- *Respect everyone's time.* Find ways of communicating that make response easy for them.

- *Don't be afraid to show your appreciation.* Send flowers. Thank people for the favors they do, in ways that respect who they are.

- *Be specific.* Don't waste your contact with a busy person by simply asking for help without having any idea what kind of help you're asking for.

Bible: "Ask and you shall receive."

Atchity: "Ask for *advice*. But ask the right people."

Self-reliance is essential to career transit. But it doesn't mean not needing people. Stephen Covey (*The Seven Habits of Highly Effective People*) calls the proper attitude "interdependence" as opposed to "independence" or "dependence." When you need help, and your own skills aren't sufficient, don't avoid the resources around you. In the years of my career transit, I've attracted an informal group I call my "advisers." We've only had an "official meeting" once, at a particularly painful economic turning point. Most of the time it's been a matter of telephone advice and support. I find that asking advice is the most natural way of making use of the human resources around me. It's the least intrusive to the person at the other end of the line. You don't need to ask him to "save you," or to "make a deal" with you, or to "give you a break." Asking for advice allows him to be his best, and do so objectively. What your adviser has that you don't have is not money or solutions or better product but *perspective.*

Persist in casting your net out, sending out daily signals to find those positive people who will help you reach the "Yes." I've found that when I'm most discouraged, and yet find the stamina to make those calls or attend those meetings, I meet the best responses. Once life sees that you're serious about your vision, she can't resist responding; and there's no greater seriousness than doing something even when you don't *feel* like doing it. Remember Ray Bradbury's advice, "Start doing more; it'll get rid of all those moods you're having." The most important thing you can do is make contact with the right people, relentlessly pruning away the negative as you forge and focus your "positive network."

Godfathers, saviors, white knights, the Little Red Hen, and clay gods

When you are lucky enough to find a "godfather" or "godmother" who shares your vision enough to support you with advice and contacts, don't make the mistake of enshrining that person on a pedestal with solid-gold status. Do not create a "savior" for yourself. If you need a savior, you're already past saving. Regarding the rescuing ally as savior gives him too much power over your goals. His reward for the rescue should be specific, not general; and it should be tangible and immediate enough so that ongoing gratitude toward him doesn't interfere with your freedom to continue moving forward toward the dream.

In the heroic quest you're undertaking through this career change, remember, *you* are and must remain the hero of your own story. You are "getting your story straight." No one can do that for you.

I always loved the fable of the "Little Red Hen," who wanted to bake bread. She made a survey of her barnyard friends and discovered that none of them were interested in helping her. They were too busy. Only her chicks wished her well. So she decided to do it all herself. When the bread was in the oven, and the aroma wafting across the barnyard, the friends began to gather around. But the Little Red Hen decided she was going to share the bread only with her chicks. The moral of this perhaps overly selfish story is that the only sure way to get what you want done surely is to do it yourself. How you deal with the "bandwagon effect" depends on your mood at the moment of victory. One successful entrepreneur took the Little Red Hen's philosophy to the extreme. He dreamed of ending his career by building a castle on a high hill with a stone wall around it inscribed with the legend: "FUCK YOU GUYS!" Another spends an enormous amount of time finding charitable outlets for his money, figuring he would rather give it to worthy causes he himself chooses than to the IRS.

Anyone can play the role of ally, dragon, kindred spirit, or white knight. But no one else can fight your battles for you. If you see every helper as a white knight coming to your rescue, not only will you risk disappointment when that person turns out to be more interested in his own story than in yours, but also you'll have disempowered yourself by turning over the responsibility for your success to someone else. The disillusionment you experience when you recognize your god has feet of clay is, actually, disappointment in yourself for having deified another human being. People who are regularly deified don't like it; it's dehumanizing to be a god. "I used to hold you on a pedestal," one of my sisters once told me. "Yes, and I never appreciated it," I said. In fact, nothing's surer to chase away a would-be ally than the feeling he gets that you're relying upon him too heavily. It's a sign to that ally that you aren't ready to be the hero yet.

Epilogue

Yogi Berra: It ain't over till it's over.

Atchity: When all else fails, run away.

When is it a good idea to stop the dream? To stop putting yourself through this torture? When you can't even find a tiny nut of hope to suck on, the dream is no longer sustainable, no longer worthwhile. Because it no longer motivates you. Then it may indeed be time to slam the door shut so you can benefit from the Spanish proverb my sister Mary once sent me: "For every door that closes, a thousand doors open."

The future opening occurs only when the present door is shut.

Once my mother came out to visit in the middle of a development deal that had been dragging on for two years and depended for its continued promise entirely on my efforts. Everyone around me thought I was crazy to continue investing my time and money and energy in the project. I asked her if she, too, thought I should give it up.

"Do you still have hope in it?" she asked.

"Yes." I said.

"Then you should continue," she said.

"Thanks, Mom. I needed to hear exactly that."

I continued, and the deal was eventually made. It's true that, as Bill Russell says, "It takes a winner to know when to change directions." But a winner will first try multiple readjustments before giving up the game. You can't win if you don't stay in.

Even if you decide it *is* time to hang it up on a particular project, before you implement your decision, leave the kitchen for awhile. Take a vacation. You'll be surprised, until it's happened a few times, what's likely to occur. While you're away,

- The decision you've been waiting for will be made: the project comes together (abandonment is normally the last step before the realization of a dream);
- You remotivate yourself more strongly than ever to continue;
- Or, most rarely, you confirm your decision to hang it up, and feel like a mountain range has been lifted from your shoulders freeing you to fly again.

Whatever occurs, in this great adventure that is your life, you will never want for dreams. If the dream that started with an outstanding logo and beautiful stationery has now become scrap paper, all is not lost. It's now part of your arsenal, and has educated your Mind's Eye to do a better job on the next dream.

Confucius: The way out is through the door.

Atchity: Every door you close firmly behind you gives you a new room to explore.

(Create a week-by-week progress chart for yourself. Here is a sample.)

CAPTAIN'S LOG for Week of _____

Week ended in: *because:*

Condition Green	
Condition Yellow	
Condition Red	

My mood (5 being highest) was (comments):

5	
4	
3	
2	
1	

GREEN LIGHTS THIS WEEK:

RED LIGHTS THIS WEEK:

Words transformed this week:

Negative	Neutral	Positive

ADDITIONS TO NETWORK:

ADDITIONS TO SAFETY NET:

ACTIVITY	HRS	NEXT WEEK GOAL:
1. SLEEPING		
2. NEW CAREER		
3		
4		
5		
6		
7		
8		
9		
10		
11		
12		

WEEK BY WEEK

Reminders, Reinspiration, and Remotivation

Week 1

Toughen up.

Use your imagination
to recognize
that most of your contacts
are going to be what "the others" call
"negative,"
and that you need to get through these
negatives as quickly as possible
to reach the only one that matters to your
dream:
the one who says "Yes."
If you've visualized that scenario in advance,
you will empower yourself
to get through the negatives faster.

Week 2

Enjoy "going to school" this "last time."

Think of your creative challenge as a
university course
you've enrolled in of your own free will
—and enjoy it!
No matter how painful
your Accountant feels it is,
remind yourself of all you're learning and
experiencing—
and that, when all works out,
you will *never* have to learn again.
"And these our present woes shall serve as
sweet discourse in our time to come."
Enjoy life.

Week 3

Stop beating yourself up!

Bad enough that the "others" ply the rod
on you for being a dreamer.
Give yourself credit instead of recriminations
for daring to go for your dream.
You don't expect instant success
and are courageous enough to live in what
"they" call a never-never land
because your hope is unflagging,
your spirit intrepid.
So, when a setback occurs,
don't blame yourself!
It's not a setback,
but another board in the raft
that gets you across the river
to the Promised Land sooner.

Pat yourself on the back.

Celebrate.

No blame.

Week 4

You're not responsible
for next week.
Today is just enough.

If today is too much,
then see your way through the next hour or
the next fifteen minutes.
Keep reminding yourself that you can do
only what you can do,
and the rest is in the hands of God, karma,
fate, or Willy Nelson.
Thoughts of next week are fine as long as
today's under control.
But for someone daring to be a dreamer,
today is *often* not under
control.
If you wanted a controlled life,
you'd be directing traffic
for the police department
counting money
behind a counter.
Trust whatever force gave you this dream
to fill in for you with all that responsibility
for next week.

Week 5

Do I have the skills?

Your ship is in a dark channel,
the storm is violent,
clouds have masked the moon,
you have no idea how deep the channel is
where you are now,
how close to shore you are,
where the rocks are, your compass is on the
blink.
All you know is that your hands
are on the wheel—
though the wheel is getting slippery.
Great.
You're the captain of this ship.
Do you have the skills to hold on to your
wheel?
The answer is Yes—
or you wouldn't be here in the first place.
Hold on.
Wait for a break in the clouds.
Keep tapping the compass.
When things get tough,
do only what's required of you
on a moment by moment basis.

Week 6

Go away for the whistle!

Don't forget, no one is tying you to the desk
or to the telephone.
You're not a 9-to-5'er.
Wait until the rush-hour traffic clears, and
take the day off.
Go to the beach. The mountains. The movies.
Bowling.
Go away until your dream surges back
into your heart,
then be thankful that you have a dream.
When you get back,
don't be surprised to find positive messages
from the future waiting for you
on the answering machine or in the mail.
Why?
Because you've *already* planted seeds.
You're not in charge of *when* they sprout.
You're in charge of *planting*.

Week 7

Don't push back!

Sometimes the best way to sell your vision
is to state it simply
and, if the response is negative,
turn your back.
If you're *always* pushing back,
you're soon going to exhaust yourself.
An old Cajun saying:
"Silence is louder dan words."
When the response is negative, you say:
"Okay, have a nice day. Bye."
Guess what often happens.
People think about it. Call you back.
If they do, great! The birth of a Yes.
If they don't, great—the loss of a No.
Win, win.
"Don't push the river, it flows by itself," says
an ancient Zen proverb.

Week 8

"Concern" is not "fear."

Avoid words like "scary," "afraid,"
"I'm terrified."
Not only are they counterproductive
to your internal trialogue.
They're contagious.
They tend to frighten your audience, too.
When something happens that is not totally
positive,
don't say, "I'm afraid that . . ."
Instead: "I'm concerned about . . ."
Concern is okay; it's a neutral word.
"Fear" is negative.
Best of all:
"There's been an exciting new development
that could be an opportunity for us."

Week 9

No self-doubt.

Eliminate it.
When self-doubt creeps into your thoughts,
words, or actions,
stop whatever you're doing.
Deal with it on the spot.
Make this your "victory habit."
After dealing with it consistently
each time it appears,
you'll find it doesn't appear as often.
The nice thing about living in your
dreamworld is
that you're completely in charge.
When you're in charge
of your method
you're in charge of your madness.

Week 10

Confront problems immediately.

"Mood" as well as "time" management
tells you that the longer you put off
the confrontation,
the harder the problems become.
Remember, they're "challenges,"
not "problems" or "fears."
Only the cowardly dreamer runs away
from a challenge;
the brave dreamer welcomes it and faces it
before Imagination comes along
to thwart him
by making the crisis worse than it is.
The barricades fall most easily at first shove.

Week 11

Take the offense (not the "offensive").

When you feel you're being ganged up on
by "the others,"
take the offense.
Don't become obnoxious about it.
Offense is not offensive.
It's dymanic, leaderly, welcome
to all those who are most comfortable
following.
When they tell you your idea won't work,
you say: "I can't believe you said that."—
and wait for that "pause of insecurity" at the
other end of the line
before you let them "see it your way."

Week 12

Victory=
plowing through negatives
& "failing fast."

Don't forget the concept of the "limited
negatives."
No matter how many await you,
it's a finite number that you must move
through to get to the Yes.
Most successful people feel that they
succeeded
by allowing themselves to fail.
Obviously, the secret is to fail fast.

Week 13

Use the "sixty-second" rule:
30 for worry, 30 for action.

Sometimes you simply can't fight worry.
The Accountant insists on it.
The moment a challenge occurs,
allow yourself 30 seconds to worry about it,
then take 30 seconds to decide on a course of
action
that turns the challenge into opportunity.
You don't need to *implement* your solution
immediately:
Give yourself some time to "mull it over."
But *make* the decision immediately
so the revision process can get to work on the
best possible solution by the time
you actually need to *do* something
(a deadline you also determine).

Week 14

Find the gift
in every problem.

This old advice is still good!
Remember your mastery over vocabulary.
"Problem" becomes "challenge" becomes
"opportunity."
You were destined to have these particular
problems you're facing
because you are perfectly able,
as the master of your dreamworld,
to deal with them.
Deal with them as a master would:
with courage, steadfastness, and exuberance.

Week 15

Assess needs.

Don't forget:
In the middle of "challenge,"
the first step in time and
attitude management
is to assess your needs,
the needs of your buyer,
and/or the needs of the situation.
Don't let imagination do this task for you.
Enlist your Accountant.
Generally, when you write the needs down,
the challenge comes into perspective
and solutions and opportunities flood your
mind.
Assess and write down needs fast.

Week 16

Take work, not self, seriously.

This is difficult advice
because no one is more intense
than the dreamer.
Yet dreamers who manage
to keep their sense of humor intact,
especially regarding themselves,
are happier than those who don't.
Take your work seriously.
Nothing is more serious than your dream.
But self-importance is simply not necessary
for success in the dreamworld.

Week 17

Learn from silence.

You don't collect information
when you're talking,
you collect it when you're listening.
Train yourself
to let the other person speak first,
and make sure you don't leave a meeting
until you've heard the other person's
concerns.

Week 18

Don't avoid the resources around you.

When you feel like you want to retreat
into a corner
and lick your wounds privately, do just that!
But don't lick forever, or your dream will die.
Reach out to the most obvious people in your
support circle
and tell them you need their advice.
They will rally to your side,
bringing perspective and solutions
you'll realize you could never have found
so quickly on your own.

Week 19

Learning is fun.

It may take a superhuman effort of the will,
but remind yourself that you're having these
particular problems
because you wanted them
and that you should be having fun
meeting their challenges.
Every day is an adventure.
If you're not having fun,
you need a vacation—
or a new career change.

Week 20

Coast.

Most career transit individuals are
superachievers
who are very hard on themselves.
The nice thing is that a new career, by
definition, implies a previous career
during which all kinds of achievements
have occurred
that continue to reap benefits for you.
If you allow yourself, under times of intense
stress, simply to "coast" for a day or so,
you'll discover the bread returning on the
waters of your former work
still provides satisfaction—
and often helps you make progress
in the new career.

Week 21

Clear your energy.

Following your gut instinct,
avoid situations, projects, and people
who make you feel that your energy will
become unclear
dealing with them.
How do you know when your energy is
clear?
You feel it.
Discover that feeling, and maintain it.

Week 22

Enjoy and savor every moment.

One of the easiest ways out of the negative
feelings that may creep into a crisis
is to stand aside from the fray
and recognize that you are good at crises.
If you're good at solving problems,
give yourself the pleasure of savoring
the problem as it occurs.
Every moment spent confronting obstacles to
your dream is a rare and unique opportunity
to enjoy
what you've been put on earth to accomplish.

Week 23

Try not to *look* driven.

You reach a higher plateau
of entrepreneurial success in self-definition
when you can appear calm and tanned
in the midst of your "worst crises."
Seeing how well you deal with strife
is what convinces those around you of your
leadership abilities.
Seeing you acting like a maniac is not
particularly confidence-inspiring.

Week 24

Pride can't falter.

You know your pride is up
when visualizing your ultimate success
makes you feel clear and powerful.
You'll avoid faltering along the way,
as unexpected obstacles attack,
by immediately visualizing the future
before dealing with the present's new
problem.
The pride that comes from that vision allows
you to go for it.

Week 25

"I can't fail at being me."

One way of eliminating failure
is by realizing that your Type C personality,
having discovered its lifelong mission and
"right livelihood,"
is automatically and by definition
successful
as long as you're pursuing
that mission and livelihood.
You can't fail at being you.

Week 26

When in doubt, push on!

Things may look dark today,
but tomorrow the sun may come out.
Even when your vision dims,
continue putting one step in front of the
other.
It's okay to work more slowly,
but work nonetheless.
Your dream doesn't require you
to be in a good mood
all the time.
It requires only that you move forward.

Week 27

Don't look back.

—except once in awhile,
in order to confirm your decision
to move forward.
The energy we can spend dwelling on the
past
is energy required for the future.
Dwelling on the past becomes the opposite
of self-indulgence;
it's oneirocide, depriving you of your dream.

Week 28

No negatives!

Remove them from your life—
all those feelings, thoughts, information,
people, and places
that bring you down.
Cancel the newspaper,
refuse to watch television,
stop talking to the "friend" who constantly
reports that "the sky is falling."
Eliminating negatives
conserves dream energy.
And energy is your dream's lifeblood.

Week 29

Ignore all "things" except to enjoy others' possession of them.

It's okay to admire the "beautiful things"
of life before you possess them yourself.
Whether in department stores
or friends' homes,
you don't have to associate worldly goods
with your present inability to purchase or
possess them.
You possess something no amount of money
can buy; your dream.
No thing can be more important than that.

Week 30

Fly as you would fly if the field were not there.

The bird flying in the fog has no clear idea
where the ground is
but doesn't allow his lack of prophetic vision to
affect his ability to fly.
The tightrope walker struts
as though the 50 feet
between him and the ground
were nonexistent.
Whatever your fear of falling,
concentrate on performing
as though you would never fall.

Week 31

Be patient.

Keeping your master seven-year operating
plan in mind,
you know that nothing that happens today,
or even this week,
can deter its eventual realization.
You may be aggravated,
but don't become impatient.
Patience is the cool required under fire,
and patience comes from firmly visualizing
the gold pot
at the end of the rainbow
from which nothing that happens today can
deter you.

Week 32

Don't complain.

Just find the right person to whine to.
Don't air your dirty laundry
with the key-holders to your future.
If you must "dump,"
do it, selectively, with a friend;
or professionally with a professional
therapist or consultant.
Grumbling is okay.

Week 33

Don't give advantage
from guilt.

You may have guilt feelings
for leaving your former career, associates,
and friends behind.
Don't let them use it against you
to deter you from the pursuit of your vision.
I know this is hard advice,
but sooner or later
you'll come to it on your own.
Start sooner and you'll get there faster.

Week 34

Count to three
before exploding.

Allow yourself to explode
when the frustrations become too intense,
but create that last little illusion of control
by waiting
until your Mind's Eye has counted to three
before exploding.
You'll discover, with this trick
that emotions *can* be controlled.
They can also be stored.
Store up the frustration for that moment
when righteous anger is required
to close on a prospect;
then count to three,
and let it out.
You'll be surprised at how much anger can
accomplish
if it's well-based and well-expressed.

Week 35

Does it matter
to the operating plan?

Whatever happens today,
ask that question before overreacting.
Most of the time, the answer is No.
If the answer is No,
deal with the new problem as a challenge,
playfully and with detachment.
Today's challenge can't take away your future.

Week 36

"The great dreamer awakens."

If you've chosen to pursue your own dream,
realize that *everything you do is important.*
You've chosen to shape life
in your own image.
Do what you feel like doing, and savor it.
If you head to the kitchen for orange juice,
savor the squeezing of the juice as well as its
drinking.
Start celebrating
the value of each of your actions
as part and parcel of the whole creative
image
that makes up "you."

Week 37

Be calm and firm.

Keep in mind the model of a leader
as one who is strong, gentle, and dignified.
Being centered on your dream
allows you to communicate conviction
to those around you.
Move slowly, accurately, and professionally.
If your energy is high,
your slowest pace
will outstrip the competition.

Week 38

No immediate reinforcement.

Give up the demand for constant
corroboration,
and work on reinforcing yourself from within
(that's the job of your Mind's Eye).
Demanding reinforcement
is energy-intensive,
not only to you the demander
but also to those you're demanding
reinforcement from.
It's also not confidence-inspiring.
Go for the long-range reinforcement.

Week 39

Don't confuse fatigue
with depression.

If you're feeling down
and you haven't had a vacation in the last
four weeks,
the first remedy is to take one—
then see how you feel.
Most of the time, moods drop from physical
and mental exhaustion;
and rise with rest.

Week 40

Maybe = no.

The sign above Karl Jung's desk read:
"YES ~~NO MAYBE~~"
to remind him that he should convert all his
"Maybe"
responses immediately into "No's"
or the world would relentlessly convert them
into "Yes's."

Week 41

Give people two chances.

You have to make a mistake the second time
to make sure it was a mistake the first time.
But when someone has disappointed you
twice,
life is too short
to continue expecting them to be among your
positive support group.
Move on.
There are plenty of strong allies out there,
if you take the time to find them.
You're wasting time in these Maybehoods.

Week 42

Don't care what people think.

You've spent enough time in your life
responding to what others think
you should be.
Now focus on
what you want to be,
and *expect* them to act weird about it.
The same people who carp and criticize
will be the first ones to congratulate you
when your level of success satisfies *their*
definitions.
So short-circuit the process.
Let what they say
go in one ear and out the other.

Week 43

No news is no news.

Don't wear your psychic energy down
with vain imaginings.
No news from "the other side"
is neither bad nor good.
It's simply no news.
Most of the time the other side
isn't even focused on
what you want them to do.
They have their hands full putting out fires.
Assume nothing.

Week 44

Enjoy the unplanned.

It's well-documented that some of humanity's
greatest discoveries
have come because creative people
found themselves in the wrong place at the
right time.
Since you've chosen a Type C life,
celebrate your freedom
whenever life freely offers you the
unscheduled opportunity—
a plane delayed overnight, a difficult detour,
a delayed business meeting.
The unexpected is your future beckoning.

Week 45

Be circumspect.

You're in the jungle.
Keep a sharp eye about you.
You can learn more from observation
than from talking.
And it's safer.

Week 46

Do something for yourself today.

Having determined to face the challenges
of a Type C life,
you deserve a special treat.
Stop for an ice-cream cone,
dally at the newsstand,
duck into an afternoon movie—
without feeling guilty about it.
Getting used to being independent
means allowing yourself
to enjoy the little luxuries
whenever you want to enjoy them.

Week 47

Give—the type-c way.

Don't feel bad that you don't yet have
the financial largesse
required to satisfy all the solicitations you
receive from a world full of charities.
Find your own way of giving back some
of the wealth.
Concentrate on giving your way,
and don't worry about ignoring the
bombardment.

Week 48

Every drop is a triumph.

Although it may be painful,
killing off smaller dreams
eventually becomes necessary
to achieving the larger ones.
Every idea or activity you decide to drop
should be looked upon as a major step
forward.

Week 49

Ignore the annoyances.

Life is filled with opportunities to go nuts
and get negative on a daily basis.
People think I'm weird to be unaffected
by every new annoyance in the air.
The truth is, I'm conserving my energy
to deal with the pursuit of my dreams.
Take responsibility for your annoyance
and recognize what it's doing to you.

Week 50

Turn rejection into linkage.

Find a way of making every No
into an open door for future sales.
In almost every business,
people buy as much from loyalty
as from product value.
They appreciate a salesperson who can take No
in a positive manner.

Week 51

Meet negatives with kindness.

It's not only better for your humanity,
it's actually less exhausting to be
understanding
when the other party is flipping out.

Week 52

Needs are not demands.

Learn to "prefer" things
rather than to "need" them
and you'll have much less nonproductive
stress.
Before you begin to negotiate
for what you want,
assess your own needs,
and those of the other party
honestly and accurately.

Suggested Reading

Atchity, Kenneth. *A Writer's Time: A Guide to the Creative Process, from Vision Through Revision.* 2nd edition. New York: W. W. Norton, 1994.

Bliss, Edwin C. *Getting Things Done: The ABC's of Time Management.* New York: Charles Scribner's Sons, 1976.

Boldt, Laurence. *Zen and the Art of Making a Living.* New York: Penguin, 1991.

Branden, Nathaniel. *Honoring The Self: The Psychology of Confidence and Respect.* Los Angeles: J. P. Tarcher, 1983.

Campbell, Joseph. *Myths to Live By.* New York: Bantam Books, 1972.

Clance, Dr. Pauline Rose. *The Imposter Phenomenon: When Success Makes You Feel Like a Fake.* New York: Bantam Books, 1986.

Cousins, Norman. *Anatomy of an Illness.* New York: W. W. Norton & Co., 1979.

———. *Human Options.* New York: W. W. Norton & Co., 1981.

Covey, Stephen R. *The Seven Habits of Highly Effective People.* New York: Simon & Schuster, 1989.

Delaney, Gayle. *Living Your Dreams.* San Francisco: Harper & Row, 1979.

Executive Health, II:XX:3 (December 1983). "Hope: That Sustainer of Man." Rancho Santa Fe, California.

Fisher, Roger, and William Ury. *Getting to Yes: Negotiating Agreement Without Giving In.* New York: Penguin Books, 1981.

Frankl, Viktor E. *Man's Search for Meaning: An Introduction to Logotherapy.* New York: Beacon Press, 1959.

Friedman, Meyer, M.D., and R. H. Rosenman. *Type A Behavior and Your Heart.* New York: Alfred Knopf, 1974.

Gallwey, W. Timothy: *The Inner Game of Tennis.* New York: Random House, 1974.

Gawain, Shakti. *Creative Visualization.* San Rafael, California: New World Library, 1978.

Gleick, James. *Chaos: Making a New Science.* New York: Penguin, 1987.

Goldberg, Herb, and Robert T. Lewis. *Money Madness: The Psychology of Saving, Spending, Loving, and Hating Money.* New York: New American Library, 1981.

Helmstetter, Shad. *What to Say When You Talk to Yourself.* New York: Pocket Books, 1982.

Houston, Jean. *The Possible Human.* Los Angeles: J. P. Tarcher, 1982.

Iacocca, Lee (with William Novak). *Iacocca: An Autobiography*. New York: Bantam Books, 1984.

Jaynes, Julian. *The Origin of Consciousness in the Breakdown of the Bicameral Mind*. Princeton: Princeton University Press, 1990.

Korda, Michael. *Power! How to Get It, How to Use It*. New York: Ballantine Books, 1975.

Kuhn, Robert Lawrence. *Dealmaker: All the Negotiating Skills and Secrets You Need*. New York: John Wiley & Sons, 1990.

Lakein, Alan. *How to Get Control of Your Time and Your Life*. New York: David McKay Co., 1973.

Mackay, Harvey. *Swim with the Sharks Without Being Eaten Alive*. New York: William Morrow & Company, 1988.

May, Rollo. *My Quest for Beauty*. San Francisco, New York: Saybrook Publishing W. W. Norton, 1985

Peck, Scott. *The Road Less Traveled: A New Psychology of Love, Traditional Values and Spiritual Growth*. New York: Simon & Schuster Touchstone, 1978.

Popcorn, Faith. *The Popcorn Report on the Future of Your Company, Your World, Your Life*. New York: Doubleday, 1991.

Richo, David. *How to Be an Adult*. New York: Paulist Press, 1991.

Robbins, Anthony. *Unlimited Power*. New York: Ballantine Books, 1986.

———. *Awaken the Giant Within: How to take immediate control of your mental, emotional, physical, and financial destiny!* New York: Summit Books, 1991.

Roger, John, and Peter McWilliams. *Wealth 101: Getting What You Want, Enjoying What You've Got.* Los Angeles: Prelude Press, 1992.

Sarno, John, M.D. *Mind Over Back Pain.* New York: Berkeley Books, 1988.

Schuler, Robert H. *The Be Happy Attitudes: 8 Positive Attitudes that Can Transform Your Life.* Waco, Texas: World Books, 1985.

Scott, Dru. *How to Put More Time in Your Life.* Rawson: Wade, 1980.

Seligman, Martin. *Learned Optimism.* New York: Knopf, 1990.

Sher, Barbara. *Wishcraft: How to Get What You Really Want.* New York: Ballantine Books, 1979.

Sinetar, Marsha. *Ordinary People as Monks and Mystics.* Mahwah, New Jersey: Paulist Press, 1986.

———. *Do What You Love, The Money Will Follow: Discovering Your Right Livelihood.* New York: Paulist Press, 1987.

———. *Elegant Choices, Healing Choices.* New York: Paulist Press, 1988.

———. *Living Happily Ever After: Creating Trust, Luck, and Joy.* New York: Villard Books, 1990.

————. *Developing a 21st-Century Mind.* New York: Villard Books, 1991.

Storr, Anthony. *Solitude: A Return to the Self.* New York, 1988.

Sun Tzu. *The Art of War,* trans. Samuel B. Griffith. Oxford: Oxford University Press, 1963.

Taylor, Harold L. *Making Time Work for You.* New York: Beaufort Books, 1981.

Viorst, Judith. *Necessary Losses: The Loves, Illusions, Dependencies and Impossible Expectations That All of Us Have to Give Up in Order to Grow.* New York: Fawcett Gold Medal, 1986.

Williams, Edward E., and Salvatore E. Manzo. *Business Planning for the Entrepreneur.* New York: Van Nostrand Reinhold Company, 1983.

Zdenek, Marilee. *The Right-Brain Experience: An Intimate Program to Free the Powers of Your Imagination.* New York: McGraw-Hill, 1983.

About the Author

Kenneth Atchity (B.A. Georgetown, Ph.D. Yale) has authored books, screenplays, poems, short stories, articles, and reviews as well as produced films for theater, television, and video. Since resigning from his tenured position as professor of comparative literature at Occidental College, Atchity has created his "dream lifestyle" around the four-part work he loves most: writing, teaching, producing, and management consulting.

His first study, as a teacher of literature, myth, dream, creative writing, and communications management was focused on the continuum from dreaming to creative thinking to communicating to new realities (leading to his co-founding of *Dreamworks: An Interdisciplinary Study of the Relationship between Dream and Art,* published by Human Sciences Press from 1980 to 1986); and then to *A Writer's Time: A Guide to the Creative Process, from Vision through Revision* (W. W. Norton). Recipient of grants and awards from the National Endowment for the Humanities, National Endowment for the Arts, Mellon Foundation, and the American Council of Learned Societies, he served as Fulbright Professor to the University of Bologna teaching American literature and institutions.

Since his career transit, he has produced numerous

films for television and video, including *Champagne for Two, The Rose Cafe, Midnight Magic, The Amityville Horror, Shadow of Obsession,* and his first theatrical motion picture, *Falling Over Backwards.* He has served as writer and on-camera for *Columbus: The Voyage of Discovery,* and is an active supporter of the Education First Foundation, which links entertainment with education. A number of his own scripts are in development as dramatic series and motion pictures.

He offers motivational lectures, seminars, and workshops for corporations and at universities throughout the United States and Europe on various aspects of myth, career-transit, time-management, and creative thinking for writers, artists, entrepreneurs, professionals, and business-people.

For information regarding Kenneth Atchity's lectures, tapes, and career transit services, or to share your career transit experience, please write, or call: Kenneth Atchity, ATCHITY ENTREPRENEURIAL INSTITUTE, 9601 Wilshire Boulevard, Suite 1202, Beverly Hills, CA 90210; phone: (213) 932–0321.